BETTING
ON
FOREVER

BETTING ON FOREVER

Billy Aronson

Illustrated by John Quinn

LEARNING
TRIANGLE
PRESS

*Connecting
kids, parents, and teachers
through learning*

An imprint of McGraw-Hill

New York San Francisco Washington, D.C. Auckland Bogotá Caracas
Lisbon London Madrid Mexico City Milan Montreal New Delhi
San Juan Singapore Sydney Tokyo Toronto

McGraw-Hill

A Division of The McGraw·Hill Companies

This book is printed on acid-free, 50% recycled paper (10% post-consumer,
40% pre-consumer).

pbk   1 2 3 4 5 6 7 8 9 DOC/DOC 9 0 2 1 0 9 8 7 6
hc   1 2 3 4 5 6 7 8 9 DOC/DOC 9 0 2 1 0 9 8 7 6

Library of Congress Cataloging-in-Publication Data
Aronson, Billy.
    Betting on forever / by Billy Aronson: illustrated by John Quinn.
      p.   cm.
    Summary: Strange-looking creatures from the past gather in their
ghostly forms for an Extinct Animal Reunion where they discuss
potential dangers to life on the planet.
ISBN 0-07-006107-6   ISBN 0-07-005829-6 (pbk.)
    [1. Extinct animals—Fiction.   2. Ecology—Fiction.   3. Wildlife
conservation—Fiction.]   I. Quinn, John (John Raymond), ill.
II. Title
PZ7.A7428Be   1996
[Fic]—DC20   96-20646
                                         CIP
                                         AC

Editor-in-Chief: Judith Terrill-Breuer
Editorial team: Robert E. Ostrander, Executive Editor
               Jackie Ball, Editor
               Sally Anne Glover, Copy editor
Production team: Katherine G. Brown, Director
Design team: Jaclyn J. Boone, Designer
              Katherine Lukaszewicz, Associate Designer   LTP3

Special thanks to Nancy B. Simmons, Assistant Curator of the Department of Mammalogy,
American Museum of Natural History, for her technical review.

Thanks to:

Judith Terrill-Breuer,
who gave my idea a home planet on which to thrive.

Jackie Ball,
my wise and witty editor,
who tirelessly shaped the manuscript as it evolved
over what seems like the past billion years.

Lisa Vogel,
my wife, who keeps my nature in balance, and our kids,
Jake and Anna, who keep our habitat packed with WILD LIFE.

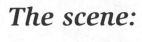

The final act:

Cast of characters:

Chapter 1

IT WAS A TYPICAL SPRING MORNING, IN A TYPICAL PARK, in a typical town. No one was in the park at the moment. Kids were in school. Adults were working, or shopping, or doing whatever they typically did on a typical spring morning.

Though there were no people in the park, the place was far from empty. Birds flitted from bench to tree to telephone pole, chirping their tuneful, cryptic messages to one another. Squirrels dashed, flies buzzed, and worms wriggled in and out of the dirt. A stray mutt wrestled with a stray sneaker.

And then, from behind a bush, came a *triceratops*.

The triceratops looked much like those you might have seen in books. The massive reptile had two long horns sticking out from the top of its head and a third, smaller horn on its snout.

But something was different. There was one thing this triceratops didn't have: a shadow. Light passed right through its body.

So did birds. A pair of sparrows flew through on their way to the bench. A rat scurried through a front foot, not even seeming to see the dinosaur.

And indeed, these animals could not see the dinosaur. They couldn't hear it or feel it. The dinosaur was a ghost.

And it wasn't alone. Out from behind a bench scampered the ghostly form of a *saber-toothed tiger*, with daggerlike fangs jutting down from its upper jaw.

And the creatures kept coming. Across the field, out from behind another set of bushes emerged a *woolly mammoth*.

With its 7-foot trunk and enormous curving tusks, the mammoth was covered with fur and had a clump of coarse hair on the top of its head.

A large-headed monkey —a *dryopithecus* (dry-oh-PITH-ick-us)— leapt out from inside a garbage can.

Inches from the monkey's toes, a shrewlike animal crawled up over a clump of grass. It was a furry little *megazostrodon* (meg-a-ZAH-stroh-don).

2

A dragonfly the size of a seagull
zipped out from the tree's branches.
This *meganeura* (meg-a-NOOR-a)
fluttered in place in the air, as down below . . .

A towering
tyrannosaurus rex
staggered out from behind
the trunk of a towering tree.

The next two creatures, appearing from behind a hill
across the field, were even odder than the rest.

The first, an *alticamelus*
(al-tee-ca-MEAL-us), seemed
to consist of a giraffe's neck
stuck on top of a camel's body.

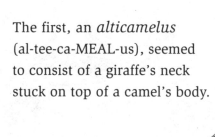

The other looked exactly like
a fictional sea monster.
It *was* a sea monster,
but it wasn't fictional.
It was a *plesiosaur*
(PLEA-see-oh-sore),
its 30-foot-long body
equipped with two sets of
flippers and a 10-foot-long neck.

More creatures began to appear, several at a time. They popped out from behind bushes and garbage cans and swing sets and trees. Some were gigantic; some were tiny. Most looked like odd combinations of animals now living. A few looked like creatures you've only seen in dreams, or nightmares.

But as different as they appeared from one another, they all had one thing in common: They were all members of extinct species. Some of their species had died out thousands of years before. Some, millions. Some, hundreds of millions.

But on this day, in their ghostly forms, they were back. The park was covered with their shadowy shapes. For a moment they just stood there, as if frozen in time.

Then they started to move. They shook. They stretched. They leapt. And then they began to come together.

They pranced, dashed, swooped, waddled, hopped,
squiggled, stomped, slithered, and scampered towards
the middle of the park, from all directions.
Quickly, they came face to face and stopped,
staring at one another in silence.
Then the woolly mammoth broke the hush.
She threw back her trunk, kicked up her front legs,
smacked the tyrannosaurus
on the back with her foot,
opened her lips wide, and bellowed,

> *"Hey there, Rexie!*
> *Since I seen you last,*
> *it feels like a million years!"*

Chapter 2

I'M A BIG OL' WOOLLY MAMMOTH WHO REALLY DOES LOVE to have herself a good time, and we sure were having ourselves a good time, let me tell you that.

We were just kicking off another Extinct Animal Reunion. I guess we hadn't had one for must have been a couple, ten thousand years. And boy, was *that* a rip-roaring heck of a lot of fun.

So this time I was about fit to bust. I was so excited to get a look at everybody and catch up with what was new on earth.

I tell you, thousands of years of not existing can be downright dull. I don't know how the others stand it, but I sure can't. Stuck out there in space. Just hanging there, a bunch of invisible particles or whatever stuck up there in the silence. If you imagine the dullest thing that could ever be, it's about a jillion times duller than that.

And it's forever—except for this one day every so often when our club of a few dozen extinct creatures (out of the billion or so out there) gets to come back. So every one of us was ready to party!

As always, everybody started off by breaking up into cliques. Everybody but me, that is. I like to mingle.

So I started off by saying hi to some folks nobody else was talking to—the oldest creatures there. The really, really old guys.

They didn't say hi back, of course, since they don't have mouths. Or, I don't think they do. Beats me what they *do* have.

I'm talking about those early little sea creatures.
Little globs is all they are. One of them has
some stringy things that look like arms.

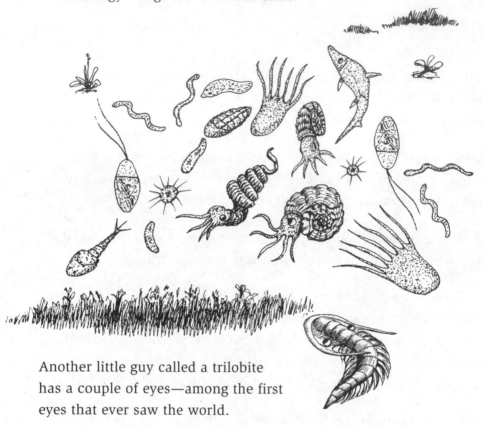

Another little guy called a trilobite
has a couple of eyes—among the first
eyes that ever saw the world.

Something like 500 million years ago, these old fellas bounced
around the floor of the ancient seas. Tiny as they look now, they
were the biggest creatures around then. They were the *only* creatures
around then!

Even though they can't do much at the party, it means a lot to all of
us that they're there. Guests of honor, sort of. Plus, it's fun to tell
them a joke and watch 'em jiggle.

Then I had a few laughs with a little crowd of early land creatures—
bugs and amphibians. How early were they? They were so early that
when they were on solid ground, it wasn't even all solid ground!
A lot of it was mushy ground!

The giant bugs used to slither up trees or buzz around the marshes.
The amphibians used to lay their soft eggs in the water, then crawl
up onto the soggy land just in time to have a bug for lunch.

I got to chatting with Meganeura, that giant dragonfly. She loves to
gossip about how everyone looks, what colors everybody's wearing.
Of course, we're always wearing the same colors. Didn't change
colors much when we were living. Don't change when we're dead.
But that doesn't stop Meg!

She started going on about my fur. Loves brown on a mammoth.
Can't imagine anything but warm, rich brown on a mammoth.
Just wild about my nut-brown fur. Just wild about the swamp-brown
tuft on my head. I never know what to say when she goes on like
that. So I told her she was looking good, too, that she was one
beautiful giant insect.

Then I moved on to a little clan of mammal-like reptiles. Never can
quite figure them out. Look like a cross between lizards and dogs!

Back in the days of the mammal-like reptiles, there were lots of
smaller reptiles roaming the earth, and a few small mammals, too.
So these guys can fit in with either crowd.

One minute they're buddying up with the dinos, wagging their scaly tails. The next minute, they're wiggling their whiskers with a bunch of us mammals.

But when I caught up with them they were by themselves, reminiscing about their golden age—hundreds of millions of years before big mammals like me were ever born—when they ruled the earth.

Then I moved on to the gang who came along *after* the mammal-like reptiles and knocked them right out of power—the dinosaurs. There were about a dozen dinosaurs gathered together, getting all sentimental about how great it was in their day. All the land in the world was pretty much one big fat continent then, and they ruled over it. Just towered over it. In those days, if you weren't a giant reptile, you were nobody. That's how they tell it, anyway.

As always, Rex got to bragging about how he could tear up this guy and gobble down that gal. Or tear up this guy *while* gobbling down that gal. Sure does like himself, Rex does.

Of course, it's been millions of years since Rex could gobble down a flea. We're all ghosts, remember. We don't eat, or drink, or even breathe. So talking about who ate who is just for laughs, like gossip.

Then I caught sight of an ancient reptile looking mighty miserable—the plesiosaur. That gal is one ton of tension.

The most self-conscious prehistoric aquatic creature you've seen in a long time. How can somebody so big feel so small? Looked just like a fish out of water.

She's not a fish, of course. But then, she's not a dinosaur either, though her name might fool you. She used to flip and flap through the sea, dipping her long neck way down to gobble up fish, keeping her distance from the dinosaurs thundering around on land.

But since most of the beasts at our bashes are land animals, I guess she feels out of place. She darts her head from one group to another, then yanks it away, all embarrassed, and hides it way up in a tree.

So I went right over and told her she looked just great. "You look just great, Plesie," I said. "The flippers, the neck, the whole deal, just great."

She pulled her head down from the tree. A little grin crossed her face. So I kept it up.

"No, I mean it," I said. "That is a fine, long neck you got there. Bet with a neck like that you could see your own butt! I've always wanted to see my own butt. Never could. Why, with that neck of yours, you could talk about yourself behind your own back!"

In no time, I had that big bashful reptile eating out of my trunk. She was chatting and cackling like the rest of us.

Then I moved on to the biggest clique of all, the group who took over when the gigantic reptiles died out, my very own crowd— the mammals.

Saber-tooth and a couple of giant sloths were having a laugh about old times, when the sloths used to get caught in tar pits. The way they told it, the sloths would be looking for berries, and they'd wander into a tar pit and get stuck in there. Then Saber-tooth would see that the sloths were stuck, and he'd creep right up to them.

When the sloths felt him breathing on their backs, they'd squirm and tug, but they couldn't get free from that mucky tar. So Saber-tooth would slit their throats with his fangs and eat the sloths right up.

This gory tale cracked up the whole gang. The sloths were laughing so hard they could hardly get the words out. "You sure were a pain in the neck," one of them said. "A real pain in the neck!"

Saber-tooth could be a pain in my woolly neck, too, sometimes. But hey, that was long ago. Having an appetite makes you do that kind of stuff. We were all a little crazy then. So what. No hard feelings. It didn't matter who ate whom or whatever anymore. We were just glad to be back on earth, slapping backs, slurping snouts, and smacking tails.

But there was one guy I didn't really feel like slurping, to tell the truth. Alticamelus, his name is. He's a yapper. Yap yap yap yap. You say something about the weather, and he starts in on some lecture about what type of clouds are in the sky and what type of birds are flying out of them and what type of dung they're dropping.

Anyway, he'd cornered a bunch of little
mammals, and they were stuck listening
to him. Trapped. He does that to you.

The nervous monkey, Dryopithecus, was
nodding and nodding—trying to keep from nodding off!
But when I caught the monkey's eye, we just grinned at
each other 'cause it was so great to be back in the sunlight.

But you know which little mammal was really grinning?
The little guy with the big name, Megazostrodon.
Donnie, as I like to call him, was sitting there,
taking it all in, smiling from one pointy ear
to the other.

I crouched way down to say hi, and Donnie told me
what he was feeling so good about. You see, of all
the mammals at the reunion, Donnie's the oldest.
In fact, he was one of the first mammals on
earth. So he got to talking about what the
world was like when there were no other mammals.

Little guys like him had to hide out all day to avoid getting
swallowed up by giant bugs and ferocious reptiles.
At night when the sun went down and it got cold,
the reptiles would have to lay low, since reptiles can't
make their own heat. But mammals can, and
their fur helps hold it inside. So the cold was
no problem for Donnie and the other small mammals.
As the big creatures slept, the mammals could creep out and feast
on plants 'til dawn.

We mammals sure started out at the bottom. A bunch of little
critters who had to creep from one hiding place to another,
cowering in fear of reptiles, amphibians, even bugs.

16

Who ever dreamed how far this mammal thing would go?

Over the ages, mammals kept diversifying, with some getting bigger and bigger. Then, after the dinos died out, we took over! Pulled a fast one, if you can call millions of years fast. That little hairy shrew was a real pioneer.

"Yes, sir. When you see a cockroach, you know you're on earth!"

Then I saw something that just blew my woolly mind. I reared back my trunk and bellowed at the top of my lungs to get everybody's attention.

The whole gang gathered round. There, at our feet, crawling along the roots of a tree, could it be? It sure was—a cockroach! *A real, live cockroach!*

There were cockroaches crawling the earth in my day. And in Triceratops' day. And in Meganeura's day. And the roaches were still kicking! . . . er, crawling!

Yes, sir. When you see a cockroach, you know you're on earth! Species come and species go, but some things never do seem to change on the old home planet.

That made us feel just super. In fact, we were feeling so fine that we started dancing. Saber-tooth grabbed my trunk and spun me around.

Triceratops leapt onto her hind legs and started boogying with Rex, who jiggled his big butt every which way. Alticamelus and Plesiosaur hopped into the action, jerking their necks this way and that. Dryopithecus and Megazostrodon clung onto Plesiosaur's tail for the rocking ride of a lifetime. And Meganeura buzzed all around overhead, zipping and flipping in time.

Soon everybody was stomping and romping and roaring with laughter—everybody except for one little creature. A new one. Hadn't seen her at the last reunion. Pudgy little bird with a big curved beak. Tiny little wings. Waddled around.

Hadn't noticed her before. Maybe she'd been hiding—sulking behind the bushes or standing rock-still to avoid conversation. But with everybody dancing, she stuck out like a sore paw.

So I reached my trunk out to her.
Beckoned for her to come on in,
the dancing's great. Instead, she gave me
this real angry look and slinked away.

"What's your problem, bird?" I wanted
to say. "You're a ghost! Lighten up!"

Anyway, when the dancing
finished we couldn't wait to go
and check out the old planet. We'd already gotten some
clues that there'd be tons of great stuff to see. There were
those big silver birds roaring way up overhead. And a
whole new kind of forest—that perfectly straight row of tall
brown trunks attached by a long, black, wiry vine.

But more than anything, as always, we were dying to see how our relatives were doing. By relatives I don't mean our immediate families—brothers, sisters, grandchildren. Heck, none of us have any of those kind of relatives left, since our entire species are long gone!

I mean members of other species that are related to ours. See, after one species dies out, other species that came from the same ancestor can live on. Over the ages these species develop and change in ways you could never imagine.

At the last reunion, Alticamelus saw a relative of his that had humps on its back! I couldn't help wondering what my woolly cousins looked like. What new parts they had, what new things they could do.

But the best thing is, as different as your relatives might be, they always look and move kind of like you. There's a family resemblance! To see your distant offspring enjoying your old neighborhood and know they're doing fine, well, that makes you feel super. It's like you haven't really left the planet. A part of you is still there.

Anyway, as we were getting ready to visit our living relatives, the gang got to one-upping each other about the good old days, and which species had it the hardest.

"In my day, we had volcanoes erupting all over the place," Rex bellowed. "If you didn't watch your back, you wound up swimming in hot lava!"

"Volcanoes?" Meganeura scoffed. "You were lucky! We had earthquakes every ten minutes. Continents were shifting every which way beneath us. You'd come home to find your nest 3 miles from where you'd left it!"

"Sounds like a picnic to me!" objected somebody else. "I remember when a huge comet came crashing right into the earth. Sent tons of dirt soaring right up into the sky. Blocked out the sun. All the plants dropped dead. Then all the small animals that ate the plants dropped dead. Then all the large animals that ate the small animals dropped dead. I tell you, a comet crashing into your planet is no picnic."

"Quit your moaning," another one put in. "So you went hungry. At least you weren't singed to death by deadly cosmic rays, like we were."

"We *dreamed* of being singed by deadly cosmic rays!" boasted Saber-tooth. "Would have put us out of our misery. You ever tried to make it through an Ice Age? With whole valleys covered with huge glaciers?"

"You all had it so easy," jeered Triceratops. "A little too cold. A little too hot. A little too shaky. Big deal."

"So what did you have that was so tough?" asked Saber-tooth.

"Him!" she said, pointing her middle horn right at Rex. "Anyone living in a world that's Rex-free has nothing to complain about."

I was getting kind of tired of all this bickering and anxious to get going. So I said, "Well, we can all agree on one thing, anyway. Since there don't seem to be volcanoes erupting all over, or comets crashing into the planet, or glaciers clogging up the valleys, and since there aren't any more tyrannosaurus rexes, creatures today must have it a whole lot better than we did!"

That's when the odd bird finally spoke. "You're wrong," she said solemnly. "Dead wrong."

Well, at least now we know she can speak, I thought. Kind of wish she couldn't.

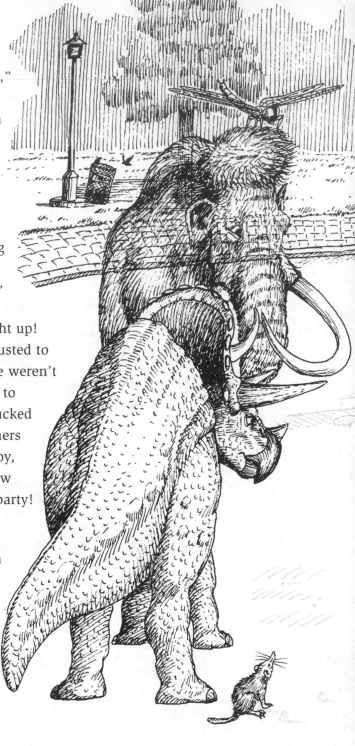

"Our relatives have it
far worse than we did,"
she went on. "It's far
worse now than when
there were voracious
dinosaurs roaming
the planet. Or
volcanoes erupting,
or climates shifting,
or deadly rays blasting
the land. In fact,
the whole planet is—"

And then she shut right up!
Like she was too disgusted to
keep going. Or like we weren't
worth taking the time to
explain. She simply tucked
her face into her feathers
and waddled away. Boy,
did that bird know how
to pull the plug on a party!

Some of us wanted to
leave her there. Go on
our trek without her.
I mean, we only had
one day here. Why
waste it on an
extinct bird with
an attitude
problem?

But old Saber-tooth couldn't let it rest. He wasn't the type who liked having his opinion challenged. "Prove it!" he growled at her. "The sun is shining. The grass is green. There are living creatures all over the place. If life on this planet is so bad, don't just sit there moping, you miserable old bird. Prove it!"

The bird looked him right in the eye and stared for a moment that felt like a millennium. Finally, she opened her beak and said, "All right, I'll prove it. But you'll be sorry."

Saber-tooth recoiled. There was something scary about this bird.

"Let's make a bet," the bird said, addressing the crowd. "I bet that by the end of the reunion, you'll all agree that your living relatives are in incredible danger . . . that life on this planet is in more trouble than ever before . . . and might well be coming to an end."

Wow. Real cheery party conversation.

"Those with the guts to face the truth . . . follow me."

With that she turned away and slipped down into
the ground. One by one, each of us followed
behind her, slipping down into the soil of our
old home planet.

Chapter 3

WHEN YOU'VE GOT A 10-FOOT NECK AND FLIPPERS, you get used to feeling ugly. Trust me. I'm a plesiosaur, and I know.

Sometimes at these reunions I find myself thinking I'd be better off dead. Then I realize I *am* dead. But somehow that doesn't make me feel any better.

I mean, all the others have legs, or arms, or wings. There's not a single flipper—except for my four.

So the whole time I'm thinking, Help! They're galloping! Prancing! Soaring! On gorgeous legs! Or graceful wings! While I just sit there.

What am I supposed to do? Slide around on my belly like a ton of live blubber?

And they're always so thrilled about travelling all over the place. They can't wait.

Well, I can wait! I'm in no hurry to be seen wriggling across the planet, flapping like a dork.

Anyway, at first when we accepted the bird's bet, I got very depressed—even more depressed than usual. Here we go again, continent-hopping, I thought. Everybody gets to watch me waddle.

But, boy, was I thrilled when she led us to our first stop. Guess what it was?

A seashore!

29

At one reunion after the next, those extinct land creatures lead us from hill to valley to plain. But never to the sea. And why should they? It hadn't been *their* home.

But this time, there we were right at the beach— the whole gang!

Just as we came popping out of the ground, so did a few thousand sea turtles. Live baby sea turtles, hatching from eggs that their moms had buried in the sand—just as sea turtles have been doing for millions of years. My old neighbors were alive and kicking.

And I do mean kicking! They scurried straight into the waves and paddled away, with no idea they were being followed by a parade of ghosts.

There's no place like home, you know? Getting back into the sea was such a thrill, it sent a tingle all the way down my 30-foot spine.

The party was taking a turn for the better, all right. And not just for me! The others were blown away by their first peek at life below the waves.

Saber-tooth and Woolly bounded from one rock to the next, checking out the scraggly plants that lined the ocean floor. Then they came to a dead stop, in front of a coral reef. "What's that?" asked Woolly. It was so great to be the expert! Clearing my throat—which took a minute or two—I explained that coral are animals and that reefs are formed over thousands of years, as their skeletons pile up.

"But look at all the stuff that lives here!" exclaimed Saber-tooth. And he was right; the place was a jam-packed paradise!

There must have been hundreds of species living on, in, and around that reef. Plants. Animals. Every inch was a home for somebody. Fish hid in cracks, waiting for smaller fish to eat, hiding from bigger fish that were looking to eat *them*. Seahorses clung to plants with their winding tails. Open-mouthed clams rested on the surface. Faceless green tubes bounced across the clams to nibble on some plant or other.

Meganeura went totally nuts over the reef creatures' colors. Blue, orange, crimson, gold, black, red, violet. The seahorse especially had Meg buzzing, as it drifted around the reef, changing color by the minute to match the nearest plant.

Baby sea turtles nibbled on the weeds growing along the surface. Bigger sea turtles with pointed bills dropped down to munch, too, but they went right for the sponge growing in the cracks. This reef had something for everybody!

Little Megazostrodon found a crack between two big chunks of coral that seemed to lead somewhere. Just as he started to wriggle in—

YAAAAAAAAAAAAAAAAAAAAAAAA!

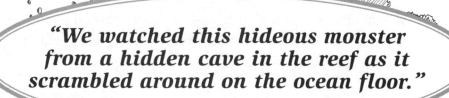

"We watched this hideous monster from a hidden cave in the reef as it scrambled around on the ocean floor."

Something sprang out at us!

Donnie flipped backwards in circles. I jerked my head away. Dryopithecus leapt right into Rex's little arms.

All together, we watched this hideous monster that had squeezed out from a hidden cave in the reef as it scrambled around on the ocean floor. The thing had eight arms, dozens of suction cups on each arm, and a fat squishy head.

And I thought *I* was ugly!

We were all surprised by this eight-armed animal. But the ancient, extinct sea creatures were the most amazed. They couldn't believe their eyes. Or feelers. Or whatever they had. That beast was about a hundred times bigger than the biggest sea creature to walk the ocean floor in their day. They couldn't get over how much time had transformed things.

You go away for a thousand million years, and poof! Change!

As we followed the bird deeper, I saw some bizarre-looking, bigger creatures I'd never seen before. There was an enormous sea beast— even fatter than I am!—floating near the surface, spitting up water from a hole on the top of its head. There was a skinny fish with a pointer sticking straight out of its nose.

But the next big fish looked familiar . . . Yes, I did recognize that awesome creature! After hundreds of millions of years, it was still going. And still terrifying! Its rows of jagged teeth were framed by a mouth that always seemed to be frowning.

When this ferocious, frowning fish came barreling toward a baby sea turtle, the turtle pulled its body inside its shell and pretended to be a rock. (Wish I could do that at parties.)

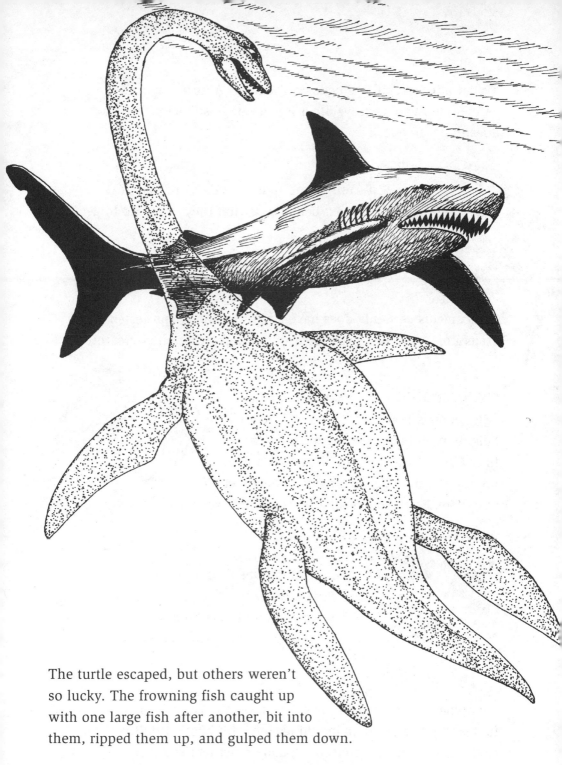

The turtle escaped, but others weren't
so lucky. The frowning fish caught up
with one large fish after another, bit into
them, ripped them up, and gulped them down.

It was pretty brutal. But so was the argument that followed.

"What utterly repulsive behavior," sniffed Alticamelus. "A creature who destroys other living things so viciously doesn't deserve to live."

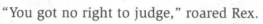

"You got no right to judge," roared Rex. "Everybody does what they got to do to get by."

"You got that right," agreed Saber-tooth.

"Alticamelus certainly does have a right to judge," protested Triceratops, "when he sees someone slaughtering other creatures."

"Well, judge this," said Saber-tooth. "Big animals that eat little animals keep a neighborhood from getting too crowded. In my day, if we saber-tooths didn't do our part, the forest would get so crowded nobody could live there. Eating other animals is a public service!"

Triceratops wasn't impressed. "If you really want to prevent overcrowding, you could build new homes," she said, "instead of snacking on babies."

"Everybody's got to eat to live," said Rex to Triceratops. "You eat plants, right? They're living things too, you know. Don't you ever think about how the poor little plants must feel when you're ripping them to shreds in your teeth?"

"What an inane argument," said Alticamelus. "Plants have no feelings. They have no brains, no nervous systems. But living creatures do have feelings. All living creatures—except, perhaps, for you."

"And bugs," Dryopithecus blurted out.

Everybody looked at the nervous little monkey.

"Well, bugs don't have feelings, right?" he asked. "I mean, along with leaves, and grass, and stems, I used to swallow the occasional insect. That doesn't make me disgusting, does it?"

"Of course not," Triceratops said soothingly. "We've all eaten the occasional bug."

"Your hypocrisy is enough to make me gag!" screeched Meganeura, zigzagging furiously from Triceratops to Dryopithecus and back. "How can you say eating animals that look like you is wrong, but eating animals that look like me is just peachy?"

"Calm down, Meggie," said Alticamelus. "We're not talking about large insects like you. We're only saying that eating extremely tiny creatures is not nearly as heinous an act as—"

"Not heinous, my tail!" yelped Megazostrodon. "Little guys got as much right to live as you overgrown slobs."

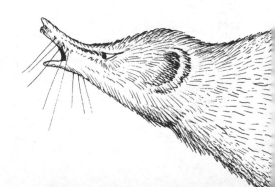

"And we overgrown slobs," bellowed Saber-tooth, "have a perfect right to gobble up tiny guys, or fat guys, or anything else that moves."

"I'll give you something that moves," raged Alticamelus, striking at Rex with his long neck, which swished right through Rex's ghostly form.

Woolly leapt in, trying to calm everybody down. "Well, now, there's no need to bicker. We all feel pretty much the same deep down, don't we now?" she said. "I mean, we can all agree that no one should eat anyone else. Unless, of course, they absolutely have to. And even then they should only eat small creatures, who are crowding up the place. Or large creatures, who are getting in everybody's way . . . uh, except for any creatures that resemble any of us here today or whom any of us care about . . ." She stopped and looked around in confusion.

Poor Woolly.
Why did she even bother?
Nobody was going to change anyone else's mind.

Just as the argument was starting to bore me, the bird caught my eye. She was swimming ahead, searching for something. And she found it: this baby sea turtle that was learning what to eat. The turtle tried to gulp down a little creature that was part blob, part strings. When it couldn't get the strings down, the turtle spit out the whole thing, and moved on to . . .

A jellyfish! I used to snack on jellyfish in my day.
I loved 'em.

As I watched the turtle gulp down its meal, remembering how good
those juicy taste treats felt shimmying down my long throat, I
couldn't help wondering . . .

What in the world is the bird so worried about?

I just didn't get it! You know? There were so many
old creatures still down there, doing fine.
And so many new creatures. And everybody
was eating! Life seemed to be doing better
than ever, down in my old home territory.

But then I saw something that chilled
me to the tips of my flippers: our first
clue that something really weird was
happening to the planet.

Chapter 4

IHAD BEEN HAVING A GREAT TIME CHECKING OUT THE ocean. Leaping. Lurking. Seeing the sights. Until that long-necked loser, that Alticamelus, made his wise-acre remark about how vegetarians have more right to live than meat eaters.

I should have ignored the moron, but I can only take so much. And his crack about the frowning fish was the one that broke this saber-tooth's back.

I mean, that frowning guy was awesome! Powerful. Swift. Really intimidating teeth. Not as scary as my fangs, of course. Whose are? But those babies sure could cut.

Armed with those rows of choppers, the frowning fish guzzled down just about anything that moved. And you know what? Good for him. That's what I say. When you've got to eat meat, you've got to eat meat, even if the meat is fish.

I get so tired of Alticamelus and his vegetarian pals passing judgment. If they're so smart, how come they're so dead? The frowning fish is alive, doing what he needs to do to keep on living.

Anyway, Woolly got me to stop snarling at the vegetarians and shake Alticamelus's hoof. And that's when I looked up and saw it.

Up ahead, floating near the surface, there was this island of . . . I don't know what. Sacks. Strings. Globs. Shiny slabs. Stuff of all colors. All shapes. All sizes. A whole huge hodgepodge, floating together in a single, gigantic blob.

"It's obviously some sort of floating reef," Alticamelus announced. "Do you recognize it, Plesie?"

But Plesiosaur just shrugged her flippers. "I never saw anything like this island when I lived here," she said.

"I know," Meganeura piped up. "It's the nest of some enormous sea creature . . . whose sense of design is abominable."

"Looks to me like a floating grazing spot," Triceratops figured. "Because, look! Sea creatures come here to eat!"

Triceratops pointed out this baby sea turtle swimming right up to the island. The turtle picked out a clear sack floating on the edge and started to nibble.

The turtle chewed. And gulped. And sucked down as much sack as it could, until it couldn't take in any more.

Then the turtle tried to spit the sack back out. But it couldn't.

As it floated around with the sack sticking out of its face, the baby turtle looked confused. Earlier, the turtle had gulped down a jellyfish with no problem. And this sack looked just like a big jellyfish. But it didn't go down like one. And it didn't seem to be coming back out, either.

What was going on? We'd already seen the turtle bite off more than it could chew, when it tried to gulp down that big, stringy fish. But the turtle could spit the stringy fish back out. No such luck this time.

So the turtle kicked and struggled for awhile. Then it just floated there. It was dead.

And as we explored the island, we found dead sea creatures all over. Small reptiles. Large fish. Sea birds. Most with chunks of the island sticking out of their mouths.

Finally, I thought I got it. "It's like a tar pit," I told the gang. "A tar pit in the sea. Where lamebrain animals would get stuck and then smart cats like me would come in and munch. Just like a tar pit, it's a natural trap. The plants in the island are poisonous, so anybody who comes to eat, dies. Then some big predator comes along and has a feast."

"But these don't look like plants," objected Megazostrodon. He had been looking closely at pieces of the island. "Nothing here looks like a leaf, a vine, a trunk, a stem, a flower . . . or anything I've ever seen growing anywhere."

"Nothing in the island looks like coral," added Plesie. "Or any shell I've ever seen that was formed in the sea."

So Triceratops asked, "But if this poisonous island is made of things that didn't grow here or form here, then how did they get here?"

"Maybe they were spit here," Rex offered. "Maybe the big guy who's going to come feast on these dead animals spits up this poisonous trap."

An island of poisonous vomit. Leave it to Rex.

So we decided to wait, to get a look at this giant predator with the huge mouth and deadly vomit. But he never came to claim his dinner.

"You'll meet the beast in time," said the odd, nonflying bird, leading us ahead.

I hoped so. I hoped she would show us this guy because I wanted to shake his paw, or flipper, or whatever, for inventing such a smart strategy.

Instead she took us to something that got me even more psyched up. A few frowning fish had surrounded this whole pack of other big fish . . . and they were swimming in circles around the pack, faster and faster.

All right! I thought to myself. A real fierce battle! Like when my gang of saber-tooths and a clan of gray wolves used to go at it. You've never seen such slashing. Or like the stories I've heard about dinosaur wars, when Rex and his brood would go up against a clan of towering opponents. Blood and guts. Fast and furious. The earth shakes 'til only a few are left standing. The strong survive.

Yes!

But just as the frowning fish were closing in, this huge web swooped down, trapped everyone on both sides of the match, and hauled them up and away.

So there was another predator—one that could shoot a web down into the waves and scoop its victims up.

"Wow!" said Rex. "Neat!"

"It's a giant spider," Meganeura guessed, "sliding over the surface of the sea!"

As we moved ahead, everywhere we turned we found the predator's webs shooting down and trapping everything in the area—all kinds of creatures—and hauling them away. Or sometimes it just left a web hanging down there, real still, so the sea creatures didn't notice and swam right in.

I could relate to the way the predator ate just about anything. I hadn't been too fussy myself. But I sure was puzzled by the way it seemed to change its mind. Sometimes, after sucking in thousands of fish and killing them, it spit most of them back out!

Or it would bite off parts of the creatures. One time, after a pack of those frowning fish got sucked up, they came right back down, still alive, with their fins ripped off.

"That giant spider up there must have huge fangs . . . and claws!" said Dryopithecus, quaking at the thought. That monkey sure does worry a lot for somebody who's already dead!

"It devours all sea creatures large enough to be trapped by its web with awesome speed," babbled Alticamelus. "Sometimes, the brutal beast strips its largest victims of important body parts and then leaves them to die slowly. This predator is far more wicked than the monster who vomits up the poisonous plants."

Yes, sir, this predator with the webs must be pretty fierce, we figured. We couldn't imagine a creature more deadly. But just then we found one. Or clues of one, anyway.

The bird led us into a part of the ocean where the water was crammed with thick, green gunk. You could hardly see your paw in front of your face.

But you wouldn't want to. Because as we moved through the muck, we realized that everybody who'd called this place home was dead. Big fish. Medium-sized fish. Tiny fish. Just floating there, all dead.

It looked like we had three guys making kills here.

The vomiting one only killed creatures who nibbled at its bait.

The web one only killed large and medium-sized creatures, while it let lots of little ones slip through.

But the one who gunked up this water got everybody.

By this point Plesie was hysterical. Her old home, you know.

"Hey, look," said Woolly to the bird, "Plesie's upset, and so are some of the rest of us. Why don't you just go ahead and spill the beans about who made this mess?"

"This mess," replied the bird, "is algae."

"But I remember algae," said Plesie between sniffles. "It formed in little green patches and got nibbled up by tiny fish. What made it go crazy like this?"

"The same creature who sucked up all those large fish with its webs," said the bird, "and vomited up that poisonous island, made the algae grow out of control."

Dryopithecus started freaking out. "You mean that right over our heads, there's an enormous mega-monster . . . that spits islands of poison from its gaping face . . . and shoots huge webs down from its gigantic spindly legs . . . and oozes deadly green gunk from its ears and its nose?"

"I don't believe it," scoffed Triceratops.

"Neither do I," said Woolly.

"How could one creature be so—er, versatile?" said Alticamelus.

"Tell us already, bird!" demanded Meganeura. "How could a big-mouthed beast armed with a bunch of webs fill up a sea with green gunk?"

The bird didn't answer. But she didn't have to, because I knew how. I knew exactly how the predator could fill the sea with algae, using nothing but webs, because of a story my dad used to tell me when I was feeling low.

"I can explain," I said. And I told them the tale.

Once upon a time, all the other large animals who lived in a forest decided to throw out the saber-toothed tigers. They were sick of the saber-tooths eating so many other large animals. So they just threw us out. (Okay, in real life, they couldn't have thrown us out. But the story's got a nice point, so what the heck, make the leap.)

Anyway, without the saber-tooths, there was nobody eating up all the other large animals. So they multiplied and multiplied.

Those animals were having a fine time, all right. But the little animals that those big animals liked to snack on weren't happy at all. With the forest swarming with large animals, the little animals got all eaten up.

At first, the large animals didn't mind having no little animals to eat anymore, because they just moved on to plants.

But they started to mind soon . . . when the whole forest began to fill up with weeds.

See, though the large animals didn't know it, the little animals had been feeding on weeds. So with the little animals gone, the weeds grew out of control.

Before long there was no room for other plants in the forest, so all the plants the large animals fed on died. And finally, all the large animals starved. Nothing was left standing in that entire forest. Nothing but weeds.

"So you see, Son," Dad would tell me, "we saber-tooths are important. We're called a keystone species—like the keystone in an arched wall that holds the whole thing up—because without us, the whole neighborhood falls apart."

"What's all this got to do with the green slime, Saber-tooth?" asked Dryopithecus, puzzled.

"The green slime in the sea," explained Megazostrodon, "is like the weeds in Saber-tooth's story."

"Right, Donnie," I said. "That frowning fish must be a keystone species. By eating other big fish, it lets a lot of the small fish who eat the algae survive. Without the frowning fish, too many big fish are left. They eat all the small fish, so—"

"Nobody's left to eat the algae," Woolly finished. "So the darn stuff goes out of control!"

"I don't buy this business about keystone species," objected Alticamelus.

"That's because you weren't one," jeered Rex. "I was. Matter of fact, with all the creatures I used to eat, I must have been the keystone-est of all! What do you say to that, you dinosaurs who spent your lives wishing I'd go away? Without me, I bet the neighborhood would have really gone gunk."

Alticamelus still didn't buy it. "Keystone schmeestone. It's all a bunch of nonsense you meat-eaters have concocted to justify your perverse appetites."

But our next stop changed his mind. We came to a coral reef that was about the same size as the first one but looked completely different.

No fish lived there. No plants. No sea creatures of any kind—except for one: sponge. The whole thing was covered with sponge. Every bit of the surface, and every crack and crevice, too. In the last reef we'd seen, there were a few patches of sponge growing among hundreds of other species. Here, sponge had taken over.

"Where are those pointy-billed turtles?" bawled Plesie. "They're the only ones who can digest sponge!"

"The pointy-billed turtle must be a keystone species down here," said Meganeura. "If those turtles don't eat up the sponge, the whole reef becomes full of the stuff and nobody can live here."

"So by killing pointy-billed turtles with its poisonous vomit," Triceratops reasoned, "the predator can kill all those creatures who depend on the reef for food and shelter."

"The predator's poison is so destructive," moaned Plesie, "that practically overnight it can ruin those coral homes that have stood for hundreds of millions of years!"

"But that doesn't make sense!" objected Alticamelus again. "Why would this predator want to harm all those creatures who lived in the reef, or in the algae-infested water? It doesn't seem to be *eating* all these dead animals. So why would it bother to concoct and carry out such a ruinous plan?"

"I know!" yelped the monkey, trembling like crazy. "This race of giant monsters up there has declared war on all the creatures who live under the sea! They're trying to beat sea animals into submission! After they've conquered the sea, they're going to come down here and squash the survivors and rule like tyrants and parade right through the water, waving their vicious webs in everybody's faces and shaking their huge, vomiting heads!"

"Whoa, whoa," said Woolly. "Let's just cut out the depressing talk. Sure we can see something's changing down here. Some new creatures are taking over, and some old ones are having a rough time. But that's what's always happened. Nobody *planned* for any of us to become extinct, but things changed."

"Look at the bright side," she continued. "We each had our turn. The early reptiles and mammal-like reptiles who used to rule made way for the dinosaurs. The dinosaurs had their fun, then got the heck out of the way for the big mammals. If the dinosaurs hadn't died out, big mammals like me probably never would have had our time at the top. I roamed and romped until my time was up, and then I moved on."

She turned to the bird. "So just cut out trying to make this new stuff seem all weird and scary! It's no different than what's been happening since the beginning of time! Now let's get back to the party."

"I totally agree with Woolly," said Alticamelus. "It's time to admit that you have lost your ill-conceived wager, my feathered friend."

"I'll admit nothing," said the bird, folding her wings. "Because you're dead wrong. You're about to see."

Chapter 5

I ADMIT I HAD ALLOWED MY SPIRIT TO BE WEIGHED DOWN by that bird's dour musings, and those of some of my companions. Predictions of vicious monsters, mass slaughter, violent upheaval, and the bird's hints of widespread doom. So as we drifted up towards the surface of the planet, on our way to the first above-ground stop on our tour, I feared we'd find the few remaining, deformed creatures scrambling across a smoldering wasteland.

Instead, we found paradise.

The bird was wrong! The bird was wrong! Oh yes, oh yes, it was time to let go all fear and shout aloud, the bird was wrong, wrong, wrong!

This new paradise was unlike any I'd ever seen on the planet. In my day the weather was cool and relatively dry, and vegetation was sparse. When we were thirsty, we had to go looking for lakes. When we were hungry, we had to search for trees. And even if we were lucky enough to find them, we had to reach way up into the branches to nibble.

But animals who lived in this forest had everything they needed right here. The forest offered convenience, comfort—and lots of company. The place was packed! Although you couldn't tell that from a casual investigation.

You see, upon entering the forest, it was obvious that we were surrounded by a plethora of plants. But only when I applied myself did I realize that we were also surrounded by countless camouflaged creatures. In one small patch of this forest, I counted as many different types of animals as there were in miles of my old habitat.

We soon realized that different levels of the lofty forest were like different, distinct worlds. The lowest level was the dark, moist ground. There we found every type of creepy crawler you could imagine: worms, snakes, maggots, beetles, 8-inch spiders. Little bugs with thousands of legs.

Many of these animals lived off the waste dropped by other animals from above. But the ants waited for no one. When they decided it was dinner time, millions of them lined up in columns as wide as Rex's shadow. Keeping in their rows, they marched straight ahead, mowing down the forest floor. They devoured other bugs, caterpillars, and even small frogs.

Dryopithecus leapt up onto my back as the wave of ants swept towards his toes.

"Don't be a baby," Rex sneered. "Besides, you're already dead."

"It *is* a disgusting sight," said Triceratops.

"Disgusting to you, maybe," Saber-tooth said. "But those birds think it's just fine."

Indeed, dozens of different types of birds had swooped down from the branches above. Along with various insects, they followed in the wake of the ants' swift march, feeding on the plentiful scraps left behind.

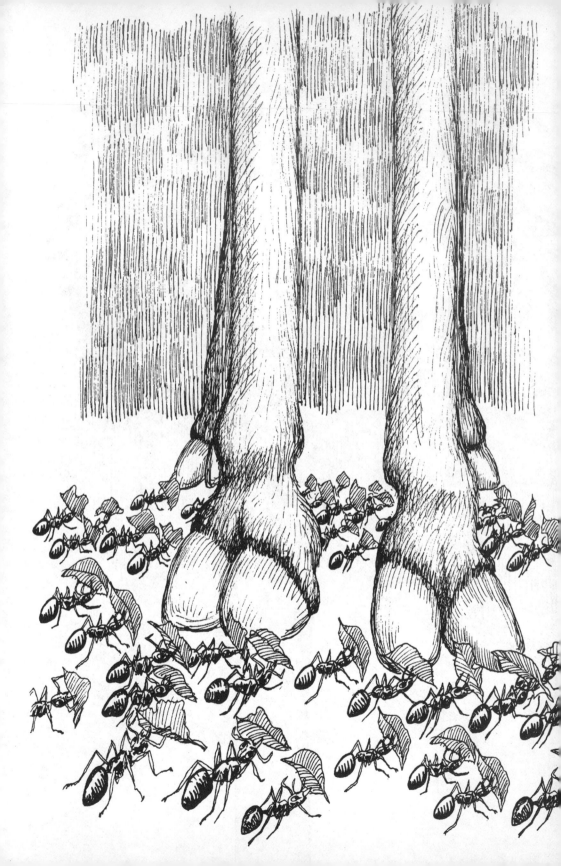

When the ants had passed, Dryopithecus slid to the ground—and leapt right back up onto my neck, quaking. "Leaves with legs!" he yelped. "Look!"

Down at my hooves, a row of leaves crept steadily along, as though they had legs!

"Those leaves aren't moving on their own," said Megazostrodon. "Teams of leaf-cutting ants ripped the leaves off plants, and now they're carrying them back to their nests."

Donnie had been examining these peculiar ants and discovered the method in their madness. "Back in the nests," he explained, "the ants cover the leaves with their spit and droppings, causing a fungus growth on the leaves that the ants can eat. These ants grow their own food!"

Who said life on Earth was in peril? These ants were eating like kings.

But my focus was drawn away from the floor when I heard Triceratops squealing about something she'd found up above. "They're sooo cute!" she cooed.

I poked my head up into the trees to find the next level, another world unto itself, where Triceratops had come face to face with her own distant relatives!

Like Triceratops, these creatures were lizards. Like her, they had scaly skin and tails. Some even had little horns. But unlike their prehistoric cousin, these reptiles were only a few inches long.

Plesiosaur slithered up the trunk to join Triceratops for a proud peek. "They look so happy, don't they, Plesie?" The two prehistoric reptiles oohed and aahed as the modern lizards stalked grasshoppers and flies.

"Those puny brats are no relatives of mine," Rex grumbled . . . until he saw his "puny" relative flick its tongue about a yard from its head to snare, suck in, and gulp down a fly. "Nice shot, Junior!" he called.

Still higher up, there was enough light trickling down for thousands of different kinds of flowers to grow. Ants came to feed on the flowers. Small birds came to feed on the ants. The birds' fluttering wings blew the flowers' pollen around, so as they ate they caused more flowers to be planted! Other birds came to feed on the fruits. Those birds' droppings contained fruit seeds, so as they flew they caused more fruit trees to be planted!

Oh, the incredible choreography of it all! But there was more.

Small mammals, equipped with wiry, mighty fingers and toes that were perfect for climbing, came to eat the fruits and the ants, too. And guess whose relative came to eat *them*?

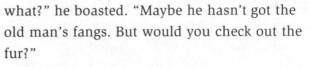

"Go get him, kid!" yelped Saber-tooth, as a fierce cat scampered up a trunk in pursuit of a doomed, small mammal. "Can that kid climb, or what?" he boasted. "Maybe he hasn't got the old man's fangs. But would you check out the fur?"

The cat's fur was sprinkled with spots, blending in perfectly with the foliage. "With camouflage like that, the kid is definitely dressed to kill!"

Irritated by the tiger's gloating, I asked Woolly to let me stand on her back so I could get a look at the top level of the forest. But even when Woolly stood on her hind legs, I wasn't high enough. So Woolly asked Triceratops to give her a boost. And Triceratops asked Rex to give her a boost. And Rex asked a brachiosaurus to give *him* a boost . . .

Several dinosaurs later, I finally was able to view the dense tangle of vines, plants, and branches that form the top level of forest, the canopy, hundreds of feet above the ground.

"Yahooo!" I heard a voice shriek as little feet scampered up my neck. "It's me—with a tail!" As Dryopithecus encountered his tail-bearing relatives, he became so overjoyed he could hardly speak. Who knew a simple rope of fur hanging from the backside could cause such glee?

Using their tails, along with their feet and fingers, to swing from one branch to the next, dozens of different types of monkeys feasted on insects, leaves, and a wide assortment of nuts.

To complete my survey, I shimmied up onto Woolly's tusks so I could poke my head through the canopy. There the sun was blazing with blinding heat. I ducked back under that extraordinary leafy roof, where layer upon layer of creature was shielded from the most intense of those rays and could live in relative comfort.

As I tumbled to the ground and extricated myself from a pool of dazed prehistoric leviathans, I began to marvel. How long must it have taken for this super-intricate system to evolve!

"Just imagine," I mused out loud, "when the first tiny organism was born in the sea, billions of years ago, that was the first step that would one day lead to this forest. Even if a planet were completely barren except for a single teeming forest like this one, then the planet would be a paradise. Even if a nasty predator is ruining the sea, clearly, my friends, on this, our old home planet, life . . . has triumphed . . ."

My eyes welled up with tears. Woolly patted my back with her trunk. The joy we all felt at that moment left us speechless, so we stood in silence, each of us finally confident that the bird had lost the bet.

And then we heard the sound.

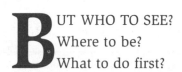

Chapter 6

BUT WHO TO SEE?
Where to be?
What to do first?

Those were the questions. So I did what I do best—I flitted. From top to bottom. Leaf to branch. Floor to roof.

I'm flighty, so they say. "That Meganeura, just can't sit still." "Always flitting, that Meg, always zipping." And it's true. For a fly, I sure am antsy.

But who wouldn't be, in a place like that forest? Among so many creatures, on so many levels, with whom I had so much in common?

Dropped in on my insect relatives, of course. On the floor. On the branches. On the leaves. On the trunks. Even peeked in at the insects living *inside* the trunks. (How they stand those cramped quarters, I'll never know.)

But even more than the bugs, I felt close to the birds. Big flyers—in stunning hues! Scarlet, blue, yellow, green. Bright bills with red bands. Striped backs. Spotted wings. Elegant. Dazzling. Exquisite.

I was having a great time when I heard that eerie sound. Roaring, buzzing, whirring, shrieking, all mixed together. Like nothing I'd heard before. Ever. And I go way back.

You could feel the sound. Vibrations, squealing. Like something from another world. A whining meteor with legs.

I followed the sound. Swooped up ahead, over miles of forest.

When the edge of the forest was in sight, the sound stopped. But I kept zooming ahead, in the direction it had been coming from.

Then I saw, down below, the creatures that had been making the sound. There was a whole herd of them. Shiny beasts, each with four loops for legs.

The beasts were asleep. Just sat there, still.

You'd sleep, too, after feasting on so many trees. That must have been what they'd eaten, because beyond the beasts were rows and rows of stumps. Not one tree left standing as far as you could see.

"Sleek frames," said Saber-tooth, admiring the sleeping monsters. "Bet they use the glare from their shiny shells to blind prey. Sharp trick! Maybe they're related to me!"

"I don't think they're related to any of us," I said. "I've never seen a creature on this planet with round legs like that."

"Neither have I," said Triceratops. "Besides, they don't seem to be made of flesh, feathers, or fur."

"Something about their parts makes me think of that vomit island," said Plesie, her huge body shuddering at the thought. "Are they related to the monster who's invading the sea?" she asked the bird.

The bird didn't answer. Just stood there. Looking sad. Looking angry.

"Now don't you go and get Plesie all upset again," Woolly warned her.

"That's right," Rex said. "Not one bad word about these shiny guys with the big appetites."

"Who could say anything mean about these guys, anyway?" said Saber-tooth. "Look at them sleeping there, so sweet and still, like a bunch of tired-out cubs."

But as we crept closer, those napping metallic cubs woke all at once. They roared and squealed as they jerked around and cruised away in a pack, accelerating at a devastating pace.

Boy, were we startled! Dryopithecus leapt deep into the forest. Alticamelus scampered away in a zigzagging pattern. I flitted in curlicues way up into the air, where I saw something that was even more startling.

"Those metallic beasts didn't eat the trees," I called back to the gang.

"Then where'd they store them," Megazostrodon asked, "in their cheeks?"

I didn't answer, because as the others caught up with me they could see for themselves: the trees that had been "eaten" were lying there in piles. Thousands of trees, just lying there, like a whole sideways forest.

"You know what you are? You're all a bunch of big-ots!"

"Your shiny creatures don't eat trees," the bird explained grimly. "They cut them down to make room for their homes and to get wood for building. And to make open areas where they can raise animals they like to slaughter and eat."

"You mean to say," said Alticamelus, "that these greedy monsters destroy the homes of countless others to build their own homes and feed their own faces?"

"Wait a minute!" objected Rex loudly. "Remember those little ants who cut down all those leaves and dragged them back to their nests to make food? You didn't call *them* greedy. But when these big shiny guys do what they need to do to feed their families, you get all bent out of shape! Big is always bad, right? You know what you are? You're all a bunch of big-ots!"

"You wait a minute, Rex," Megazostrodon piped up. "Size is not the only difference. When the ants cut down leaves, other leaves grow right back in their place. But when these creatures cut down trees, the ground turns to dust, and nothing can grow there."

To prove his point, Megazostrodon scampered ahead through caked, dry dirt that puffed up beneath his feet.

"Donnie's right," said Alticamelus. "Without that canopy of leaves to filter out the intense rain, sun, and wind, the soil is flooded, scorched, and blown away."

"So those metal monsters reduce paradise to dust!" yelped Dryopithecus.

"Wait a minute, now, before you get all hysterical," said Rex. "Inside the forest, I saw birds eating fruit, seeds and all, then flying away from the forest. And as they flew, they scattered seeds in their droppings. Those seeds would plant new trees, right? So as long as the birds keep planting, let the shiny guys keep munching! The system works!"

"The system *doesn't* work," said Alticamelus. "Because the monsters are destroying it, not participating in it."

"How so?" asked Saber-tooth.

"Put your paw on that stump," said Alticamelus. "It's warm! Still burning from the monsters' hot breath. So the beasts must have yanked down and piled up those thousands of trees in the last few hours!"

Awesome thought. But hard to dispute.

"It takes hundreds of years for new trees to grow so tall," Alticamelus continued. "If these voracious monsters chomp down forests that quickly, how could the birds possibly keep up? Even if they wanted to, with fewer and fewer trees remaining, where would they perch to eat their fruit?"

"So Dryopithecus was right," said Triceratops. "Every time one of these metal monsters has its feast, thousands of animals are left homeless." She turned to Rex. "Not even *you* could kill thousands of living things in a single lunch."

"Could too!"

"In your dreams!"

"Now there's no need to start talking about killing," said Woolly. "A lot of folks will have to move, sure. But I keep telling you all, you gotta be adaptable. Me and my family were moving all the time. Every time it got too cold in our neck of the woods, we'd just pick up and move on. Didn't kill us."

I adore Woolly. Big, loveable fur-face. But those insensitive words of hers left this fly totally bugged.

"Well, excuse the rest of the animal kingdom," I said, "if not everybody's as happily homeless as you."

I'd been checking out those forest creatures up close. And it sure seemed to me they were suited for where they were—and wouldn't survive anywhere else.

"Away from the forest, their colors would be all wrong!" I began. "In here, they match their surroundings perfectly and can stay hidden from enemies. Out there they'd stick out like sore thumbs and get gobbled right up!" But color wasn't the only thing. "Some animals make nests in tall trees to keep their eggs safe from predators on the ground," I continued. "What happens to them if there are no trees? Their babies will be history before they're born! And what about the creatures who get around by swinging and climbing? They can't just start walking upright overnight."

I flew over to Woolly. "Your woolly ancestors didn't get good at roaming overnight," I told her. "They got more and more fur over hundreds of years, one generation at a time. They developed certain muscles, skills, and colors gradually, too. But those metal monsters aren't giving the forest creatures centuries to adjust. The monsters are throwing them out without a moment's notice. They'll die."

Woolly turned away. I felt bad. After all, she'd just been trying to put a nice face on things. But when things are really ugly, putting a nice face on them doesn't help. Better to just let the ugly face show and deal with it.

Which is what we did. We sat there thinking about all those comfortable forest creatures being thrown out of their homes to die . . .

Until Rex started fidgeting. "Oh, what's the big deal!" he bellowed. "So a few shiny guys are stamping out a bunch of tiny critters. Yes, tiny! That forest is so overgrown with trees that decent-sized creatures would be afraid to come in. They'd bump their heads every time they hiccuped!"

He turned to the bird. "Enough with the piddling problems of the planet's puniest. If you're going to convince me there's anything wrong on the planet, take me to where the big beasts are on the loose. Bring on the giants!"

And so she did.

Chapter 7

F INALLY!

Beasts you could see without squinting. Hear without straining.
Smell without sniffing.

By having the bird bring on the giants, I'd put an end to her
tiresome Tour of the Tiny. The jungle she led us to this time wasn't
nearly as thick with trees as the last one, so there was lots of room
for the big guys. The creatures here were so hefty you could actually
imagine hanging out with them, getting to know them, and ripping
their guts out. Having a real party!

They were awesome, all right. But make no mistake: I would have
ruled anyway.

This large cat lumbered by, shaking his mane in my face, strutting
around like he owned the place. "Yo, pal!" I roared at the cocky cat.
"Who died and made you king?"

He stalked a pack of black-and-white striped horses. He leapt.
He ripped. He feasted.

Nice moves, I thought. Not a bad set of weapons. Good teeth. Good
claws. Passable roar. Still, I could have eaten the cat for breakfast.
Ripped him in half with a chomp. Guzzled the guts, spit out the
mane. Nice morning meal.

With him out of the way, I'd rule this jungle, terrorizing my many worthy foes. And check out the jumbo-sized servants I'd inherit: those megaton gardeners!

They were the homeliest of Woolly's relatives I'd ever seen. Gigantic ears flapping around. Heads almost hairless. Whole bodies almost hairless! Saggy skin hanging in wrinkly folds.

But blood's thicker than fur, I guess. Woolly nuzzled right up to the wool-less mammoths, got all teary-eyed.

These big-eared, bald guys had one thing in common with their Woolly cousin: they were crazy about plants. As we watched, they kept barrelling into trees, knocking them down so they could munch on leaves. They were pruning the jungle, letting in sunlight, and keeping the place from getting overcrowded with trees. Performing a real public service, you know? So even though these guys looked real juicy and tender—and came in extralarge portions—I decided that if I ruled here, I'd definitely spare my hefty gardeners. (Except maybe on my birthday, when I really like to pig out.)

We traveled a long way, into a deep part of the forest, where we saw some big, hairy guys in the trees. Most massive apes you ever saw. Their arms were lined with muscle, their chests were rock solid— and they knew it. Loved to pound those chests with their furry fists.

"Show-offs," scoffed Alticamelus.

"If you've got it, flaunt it," I defended, thinking about how I'd eat them. They wouldn't go down easy. I'd rip off the heads first. Gulp down the brains. Spit out the skulls. Then I could take my time gorging myself on the thick, juicy muscles.

Meanwhile Dryo was
leaping around like a
lunatic, pointing at a couple
of his other relatives as they pulled off a
neat little trick. They were sticking twigs
into the cracks in tree trunks to pull out
little bugs, which they then slurped up.

"Would you look at this?" he yelled. "I spent my life trying to come up with a way to get bugs out from the trunks. I tried sticking my tongue in there. I tried sticking my *toe* in there. I even tried curling up into a ball so the bugs would think I was a glop of dung and come feast on me. Stayed perfectly still for a week once, but the bugs never bit. But my ancestors have found a way to stick it to the bugs . . . and dig out an endless supply of snacks! They're the geniuses of the jungle!"

Geniuses, huh? I'd never eaten a genius. But I try to be open to new things.

We made our way out of the deep forest back into the same kind of grassy place we'd been before. Alticamelus immediately started prancing around with a spotted animal whose long neck stretched way up into the trees. Towering, quick, graceful creature. Height of a dinosaur, poise of a deer. (I'd slash the throat, open the belly, help myself.)

Triceratops studied a thunderous quadruped with horns kind of like hers. Everywhere you looked there were hulking beasts. And every one of them impressed me as a privilege to battle, and an honor to eat.

But it was a relative of Saber-tooth's who really blew me away. Gold-colored guy with dark spots. He had his eye on a long-horned antelope grazing in the open. But instead of approaching the antelope, this cat kept his cool. He just watched, crouched, totally silent, not moving a muscle. Didn't even seem to breathe, for what seemed like minutes.

"I'd never eaten a genius. But I try to be open to new things."

Talk about patience! After about three seconds I'd have cracked up and gone ahead and charged the dumb antelope already.

But this guy just sat there, frozen.

So I was thinking, when's he going to start creeping closer? I mean, he's still half a diplodocus away!

But the cat never did creep close.

He didn't have to.

Because suddenly he leapt. That's right, leapt the whole distance . . . roaring his head off as he soared through the air . . . and landed right on the antelope. He grabbed it by the throat, wrestled it to the ground, and strangled it. Then he whipped out these enormous claws, ripped out the guts, and started to munch.

The kill was over in a flash. It absolutely blew me away. And you know what? It blew the rest of the gang away, too.

"So what do you say now?" I roared at them. "Those of you who like to dump on big creatures still find this stuff disgusting?"

Nobody answered. From the mild-mannered Mammoth to the meek Megazostrodon, I knew they couldn't help being thrilled with that display of awesome power.

"I think you're all downright proud of modern, full-sized animals," I continued. "And you should be! They're mighty, swift, and ferocious! You don't see any shiny-backed predators driving *them* from their homes. Or any web-shooting monsters swooping *them* up and spitting *them* out. With these big guys ruling the land, I predict this jungle of the giants will thrive and grow, just like my valley of the dinos did, for hundreds of millions of years!"

And then, pop!

There was this popping sound. And down he went. The cat went right down, just like that.

Was he faking it? Baiting somebody? I wondered.

We gathered around to check.

He wasn't faking. He wasn't breathing. He was as dead as the antelope. And there was this puddle of blood seeping from the side of his face.

Weird. Very weird. All that power, all that grace and might. Down. In an instant.

Everybody started in with their theories.

"Struck by a tiny meteor!"

"A plague's sweeping the jungle, I tell you."

"A poisonous, blood-sucking bug."

"No, no, it's a predator who's invisible!"

I tried to listen, but their words swirled around and around in my head. I felt dizzy and sick. All those smarts and skills, cut down with a pop.

Some new kind of snake did it, a snake with wings, that's what I thought. A snake who could blast through the air like lightning and dart out of sight. A killer so swift you couldn't catch him, or dodge him, or even see him.

For the first time, I considered the hideous possibility of a creature more deadly than me. More deadly than anybody.

The others were begging the bird to explain what had just happened.

But you know, I didn't want to hear. I'd seen too much already. I wanted to go back to a past reunion, or wake up in another age altogether.

Anyway, the bird wasn't talking. She just motioned with her beak up ahead at some animals coming out from the bushes to check out the dead cat. Monkeys they were, more or less. Tall, scrawny chimps. No fur, except for a patch on the head. Walked on two feet, straight up. A few toted long sticks, like Dryo's relatives who pulled bugs out of trees on twigs, so I figured they were geniuses.

Chapter 8

ON ONE LEVEL I WAS GLAD, TO BE HONEST WITH YOU, when the spotted cat went down.

Sure, I also felt sad and horrified, as everyone else did. But deep down, I couldn't help feeling a little twinge of glee to see Rex humbled.

I wanted to shout, "Thank you, invisible predator, whoever you are! Thank you for reminding us that no matter how strong a creature is, somebody stronger is always going to come along. Thank you for reminding us that anybody who kills can someday be killed. Thank you for getting Tyrannosaurus Rex—finally—to shut up!"

I strolled along with Woolly as our weird bird guide led us away from the jungle through a big, dry area. Boy, was it hot! Sweltering. As I looked out across the expanse of scorched ground, I saw few plants and no water. But there were animals all over the place! Little mammals scampering around. Reptiles. Birds. Big cats. More antelope. "What do you suppose they drink," I wondered aloud to Woolly, "sand?"

But then my answer came thundering along. A herd of Woolly's big-eared relatives showed up to make water appear in the middle of a dry plain.

Guided by some kind of mysterious special sense, they zeroed in on a particular area in the dirt. After they used their special sense, they started using their brute force. They rammed their tusks into the ground to loosen the surface and scooped out enough ground to clear away a watering hole!

As they slurped up water in their trunks, all the other animals came around. From the biggest cats to the tiniest lizards, they showed up from all directions to get a few drops to drink.

> *"When Woolly started sniffling, Saber-tooth awkwardly patted her back with his paw. "I know," he said. "It's a jungle out there."*

Woolly was tickled pink. "Would you look at this?" she shouted. "Drinks for everybody, courtesy of my cousins! Are my kin a keystone species or what?"

Maybe they were. One thing was for sure: without them to find and dig up the water, the other animals would be a lot thirstier. Which is why we were especially horrified by what we saw just beyond the watering hole. Four of the modern mammoths, lying side by side, their corpses swarming with flies.

Even Rex was startled by the grisly sight.

"Even *I* never killed four beasts that size at once," he admitted.

"Because you couldn't," I muttered.

"Could, too!"

"Dream on!"

Donnie examined the creatures' heads up close. "Looks to me like the work of that same popping predator who got the cat," he concluded. "Same little pools of blood dripping from their heads."

When Woolly started sniffling, Saber-tooth awkwardly patted her back with his paw. "I know," he said. "It's a jungle out there."

"But why did this predator have to go and kill my relatives?" she wailed. "He couldn't have been hungry, because he didn't eat them. He just left them lying there."

"He didn't leave *all* of them," said Donnie, pointing to holes on the sides of each big-eared face. "Looks like this predator has a special taste for tusks."

The little guy was right. Before leaving the bodies to the flies, the predator had yanked out every one of their tusks.

"Maybe this predator is related to that monster with the webs," Plesiosaur said. "Remember the one who ripped the fins off the frowning fish, and then spit the rest of them back out?"

"Looks like there are picky eaters afoot!" I said, trying to keep the conversation light. "My gorgeous horns wouldn't last a day in this neighborhood, I tell you."

Even as I tried to appear casual, I was disturbed. In my day, if a predator went to all the trouble to kill somebody, you can be sure he wouldn't just take a couple of slivers and leave the rest. It's hard work killing a big creature! If you're not really famished, why bother?

"Cheer up, Woolly," called Meganeura from above. "There's another whole team of your cousins searching for water up ahead!"

As we followed this new gang of Woolly's relatives, she perked right up. Until . . .

They walked straight into the world's widest hive. Well, I don't know if you'd call it a hive. It was a cluster of nests. But these nests had tops!

The area was teeming with tall chimps, like the ones who came to see the dead cat. It was absolutely swarming with them! Tall chimps here. Tall chimps there. They rushed in and out of those enclosed nests of theirs, cramming the whole area.

As I watched, I had to admire them, really. So frail, scrawny, and vulnerable. I couldn't think of a mammal with punier muscles. Or less fur! Their flesh was so flimsy and bare, they had to cover it up with different materials.

But in spite of their obvious shortcomings, the tall chimps had survived somehow. They probably compensated for their frailty with their—as Dryopithecus would call it—intelligence. They waved sticks around, carried things from one place to another, put things in piles.

On the other hand, they had done something that wasn't too smart. They'd built their nests right in the middle of Woolly's cousins' path to their watering hole.

Now the sight of these hefty mammoths coming towards them sent the tall chimps into a panic. They shrieked, scurried in all directions, and threw whatever they could find at the giant beasts.

But the tall chimps' hysteria made the mammoths panic.
And bellow. And charge. And trample the tall chimps' nests.

And boy, did that make the tall chimps mad! A couple of them pointed sticks at the charging animals. The sticks made those popping sounds . . . and the mammoths dropped to the ground.

And suddenly the pops made by the sticks started thoughts popping in our brains.

"So it was tall chimps that killed that cat," said Rex.

"And it was tall chimps that killed the four mammoths in the desert," I said.

"And it was tall chimps that killed these innocent creatures just now, right before our eyes," said Woolly. "Innocent creatures who were trying to find water."

"Well, what do you expect?" Dryopithecus exploded. "Your relatives came barrelling right into my cousins' neighborhood!"

Woolly was indignant. "Why did your cousins have to build their homes there?" she asked. "Right in the middle of my relatives' path to their watering hole!"

"Creatures build anywhere they want," said Rex. "As long as they can defend their territory—which the tall chimps can. Obviously."

"Say what you want about survival of the fittest," said Woolly. "But those tall chimps didn't have to kill my cousins to steer them away from their homes."

"They didn't *have* to," said Alticamelus, "but the tall chimps panicked. It's quite natural. They felt their homes were in danger, so they lashed out."

"Some creatures sting when their homes are invaded," agreed Meganeura. "Others bite. I guess the tall chimps go for their sticks and pop you."

Woolly was in no mood to forgive. "And I suppose they felt their homes were being invaded by four animals?" she asked. "And by one lone cat?"

"All right, maybe my cousins made a couple of goofs," admitted Dryopithecus. "They're a new species, right? Maybe they're still figuring out just when to pop and when not to pop."

"They might not be all that new," said Saber-tooth thoughtfully. "I'm starting to remember some scrawny apes from my day who looked like the tall chimps, except furrier. They carried fat sticks that they'd bop us on the heads with."

"I remember those apes too," said Woolly. "Hairier, shorter versions of the tall apes. They'd smack us with fat sticks. Or stab us with sharp sticks. Didn't like 'em much then either."

"The species sure has come a long way in a few thousand years!" said Saber-tooth. "Those fat sticks could smart a little, but with the popping sticks, tall chimps can kill big animals without even getting *close*."

"You mean they can murder anybody without even getting their hands dirty?" said Woolly angrily.

Dryopithecus curled up into a ball. "Enough about my cousins already!"

Alticamelus rushed to his friend's defense. "When different powerful creatures cross paths, there's bound to be the occasional misunderstanding, the odd flare-up, a few incidents—"

"Nothing that I'm showing you has happened *occasionally*," the bird finally burst out. "These primates and their deadly sticks clash with big animals around here every day. The primates always win. The big animals are losing, in a big way. And so are all the other creatures."

The bird led us to another jungle, beyond the tall chimps' area. What we saw there proved that those mammoths were a keystone species, all right. And not just because they sometimes helped others find water.

This jungle had become overcrowded. The trees were growing so close together that other plants were forced out. And that meant small animals who ate those plants would go hungry. And bigger animals who ate *them* would go hungry, and so on, and so on.

Those relatives of Woolly's are the only creatures strong enough to pull down trees," the bird explained, although we had already figured it out.

Plesiosaur's eyes began to well up with tears. "It's like that algae-infested water," she said. "By wiping out a keystone species, the tall chimps might be wiping out entire neighborhoods."

"It reminds me of that thick forest where the truck creatures lived," said Meganeura. "Only opposite. There, the truck creatures destroyed a neighborhood by removing trees. Here, the tall chimps have destroyed a neighborhood by letting there be too *many* trees."

"But it all adds up to the same thing," I said. "The balance is upset and the whole neighborhood falls apart."

Dryopithecus started chewing his long fingers and shivering.

"Hold on now, friends," said Alticamelus, trying again. "Surely you'll grant that any similarities between those dreadful calamities at sea and in the forest and the little mishap in this jungle are purely coincidental. By lumping them together, you're making it sound as though Dryopithecus' skinny little cousins are responsible for all the evils of the planet!"

"We're sorry, Dryo," I said. "We didn't mean to make it sound that way."

"Didn't we?" said the bird. "Speak for yourself!" She turned to address the group. "It's time to put an end to your pathetic ignorance and confusion. So hold on for a high-speed tour of a planet that—though it was once your home—you will now find totally unrecognizable."

Chapter 9

IT WAS CHILLING. IT WAS DISGUSTING. IT WAS ALSO REALLY humiliating!

I mean, the sight of animals being brutalized across the entire planet sickened us all. But for me it was also really embarrassing, since the creatures doing all the brutalizing were the tall chimps—my relatives!

You know how it feels when a relative of yours does something really rude or idiotic? You want to climb a tree, curl into a ball, and hang upside down by your toes, right? Well, imagine how it feels to have a relative of yours going around killing just about everybody on the planet.

We're talking major embarrassment.

At each of the first three stops on the tour, we'd seen animals in trouble. We figured those places had been picked because those animals had it especially rough.

We were wrong. If anything, those creatures were lucky. As tough as things were for them, at least they got to live with lots of other animals.

As the bird led us around the planet on our high-speed survey, we saw tall chimps everywhere, but few other creatures anywhere. The

stray creatures we *did* see lived like fugitives, scrounging, hiding, on the run, hungry.

Everywhere we went it was the same. Tall chimps doing, tall chimps building, tall chimps going . . . and everybody else getting trampled, cleared away, and crushed. None of us had ever seen anything like it: one species in command of the entire planet.

"Your relatives are squashing mine!" Triceratops yelled at me. We were in a marsh, where tall chimps had cleared away all the plants and built paths where they could ride in their shiny monkey-made beasts. But as they rode, the tall chimps didn't seem to notice that their shiny beasts were squashing one tiny reptile after another.

"Anybody can build wherever they want, right?" Woolly taunted Rex. "Everybody thought that was a fine rule when it was my relatives getting pushed out of their homes and slaughtered. How do you like seeing your poor little cousins getting whacked?"

"It is unfortunate about those lizards and snakes," said Alticamelus. "But we all know that when an environment changes, creatures who aren't well-suited must die out, so creatures who are better suited can take over. That's how evolution works."

"Not well-suited?!" raged Triceratops. "The little reptiles are perfectly suited for that moist, marshy area!"

"Not any more," said Alticamelus. "Now that the tall chimps are coming through with their swift, shiny beasts, your relatives are simply too slow."

"And I suppose swift creatures like you would do just fine?" asked Woolly.

"Of course we would," Alticamelus boasted. "Just look at that speedy, nimble deer."

The bird had brought us to a monkey-made path that led right through the woods. "Watch as the tall chimps come roaring along in their shiny beasts," said Alticamelus. "See? The deer have no trouble leaping right by, one, after another, after an—"

Thud. Crash. Squash. Oh, dear.

Alticamelus wished he hadn't spoken. I wished I hadn't been born.

Meganeura, however, was perky as ever. "Oh, well," she said, "when the going gets tough on land, the tough take to the sky!"

Overhead, things did look fine. Big birds with enormous wings soared effortlessly along, free from the dangers below.

Until they got hungry. Then the birds had to swoop down to pick up a rodent for lunch.

When they swooped down in chimp-free areas, the birds were fine.

But chimp-free areas were few and far between. When one of these large birds swooped down in the vicinity of a tall chimp, the chimp panicked, pointed his stick, and popped.

As the bird came crashing down, Meganeura perched on a rock and stared at the feathery corpse. "No one," she muttered, "has ever had to survive in a world like this."

"I did," said Megazostrodon. "It's like in dinosaur days. When the monsters are on the march, you just have to lie low. Stay in when they're out, come out when they're in, you'll be fine."

We trooped along until Donnie found a creature with which to illustrate his point: a small, black-tailed rodent that was poking its head out of a tiny, secluded hole. After checking in all directions, the rodent scampered out and charged across the plain to an enclosed area where horses pranced. Then, after once again checking in all directions, the rodent sniffed around and gobbled something that looked like pebbles on the ground.

Then the rodent died.

"Well, we can't blame Dryo's relatives for that," said Donnie. "There are no tall chimps anywhere around."

Boy, was I relieved. At last, a death that wasn't even remotely my fault. Yippee!

But then, guess who showed up? A tall chimp came to sprinkle more of those deadly pebbles. My intelligent ancestors had found a way to kill while taking a nap.

Donnie stared in disbelief. "That's no way to treat another mammal."

But that was just how the tall chimps treated plenty of other mammals. As we sped around the land, we could see in devastating detail how anybody who came anywhere near the chimps—from big bears to sleek wolves—was poisoned, popped, or caught in a bone-shattering metallic contraption.

"Your cousins are determined to have the whole planet to themselves," Saber-tooth said to me.

"Just a small part of it, really," corrected Plesiosaur.

What was this? Just when everybody else was so angry they could hardly look at me, the most depressed member of our group had been seized by a sudden burst of optimism! For the first time in my life, I wanted to kiss a marine reptile.

"I don't know what you're all so worried about," she continued. "Only a small part of the surface of the planet is land. Most of it's water. Since chimps are land creatures, the other animals should do what my ancestors did to escape from the mighty meat eaters of their day: Move to the sea! Grow some flippers! Learn to swim!"

"Move to the sea?" asked Woolly. "You saw the terrible stuff the monsters down there were doing!"

"Those monsters couldn't possibly be as bad as the tall chimps," argued Plesie.

But as the bird led us zooming over the sea, we quickly realized that the monsters who ruled the sea were every bit as bad as the tall chimps. Because they were the tall chimps. The sea was packed with them.

In the shallow areas they bathed, played, and scavenged the coral reefs. They moved across the deeper parts of the sea, too, on floating beasts. In some cases, big fish collided with the floating beasts and were killed. In other cases, the killing wasn't quite so accidental, as tall chimps tossed out webs to haul in thousands of sea creatures.

"The tall chimps were the fin-rippers!" exclaimed Plesie.

"And the web-droppers scooping up keystone species!" said Triceratops.

> ## *"For the first time in my life, I wanted to kiss a marine reptile."*

But the most brutal sea killing was done by tall chimps who weren't in the sea at all. They killed from the shore, without even knowing it!

You see, the chimps on shore liked to wrap things. And unwrap things. And peel things. And rub on things. And squeeze out things. And pour out things. And tie up things. And to do all their wrapping and pouring and tying, they used all kinds of materials selected and crafted with incredible intelligence.

But once again, intelligence was a double-edged banana.

After using these materials, the chimps left them on the beach. Then the waves swept the stuff out to sea, where it all washed together to form islands of garbage.

"They're the vomiting beast, too!" gasped Alticamelus.

At this point my slender cousins were looking like the deadliest creatures who ever lived, and my extinct friends were wishing I'd never been born. All I was wishing was that I'd been born as someone else.

Then—suddenly—hope!

As the bird led us back over land, I spotted a towering creature below, much larger than the chimps—and much more deadly. It sat there, still, its arms curled around a lake . . . spitting black smoke into the sky.

"In time, those deadly fumes will fill the clouds, come down in the rain, fill the lake, kill the fish, and then kill the animals that eat the fish," intoned the bird, "In a merciless cycle of death."

I could hardly hide my relief. "Yes, but it won't be my relatives' fault!" I yelped. "The planet's new reigning villain is that towering monster filled with poison, filled with anger, filled with—*tall chimps?*"

Yes, even as I spoke, a stream of tall chimps walked out from the mouth of this, yet another monster of my relatives' own creation.

"Well, who says they're chimps, anyway?" I asked, desperate to distance myself. "Maybe they're not even primates. Couldn't they just as easily be reptiles like Rex and Triceratops, who've stuck on some fur, smoothed over their scales, and lopped off their tails? Or giant insects like you, Meg, who, after being blasted by hideous rays from space, have been mutated and deformed beyond all recognition? Or birds who shed their feathers? Snakes who sprouted arms? Upright dogs having a bad fur day?"

No one seemed willing to consider these alternate explanations. In fact, nobody was even willing to look at me anymore.

And who could blame them? As we looked even more closely, we realized that some of my relatives weren't content with just killing other creatures. They also had to wear them! We saw tall chimps wearing the skins of large cats on their backs and wearing the skins of reptiles on their feet or around their bellies. These relatives of mine were getting pretty tough to defend. But I didn't stop trying.

"Okay," I admitted, "so maybe creatures of this one type have done a lot better than all the rest. And maybe, as they gain power, they take power away from other types of creatures. And maybe you, and my friends here, and even I, might not think that's very fair. But when has survival been fair?"

I turned to face the bird. "So I suggest you either prove your point—that life on the planet is in more danger than ever, maybe coming to an end—or admit you've lost and let us get back to some wild and crazy dancing."

Unfortunately, of the two options I offered, she chose the first.

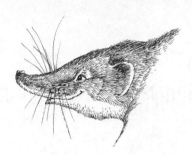

Chapter 10

WELL, IT'S ME, DONNIE, HERE TO TELL YOU WHAT THAT odd bird said to us when she finally told us her story.

Sure, I'm just about the size of a pinecone. But I've got a memory the size of a mountain. Remember every word of the odd bird's speech, I do.

And what a speech it was.

Made the fur on my neck stand on end. Made my whiskers twitch. Made my toes curl up. Made my ears shiver. Made my tail stick straight up, stiff as a tree, and just stand there, stock-still.

Riled me, it did.

It went like this:

I belong to a species of nonflying birds called dodos that went extinct just a few hundred years ago. Though we're related to birds that can fly, at some point my ancestors wound up on an island where life was so easy they didn't need to fly. What made it easy? There were no predators.

With no predators, we never had to flee. So over the ages our wings got smaller and weaker. We didn't have to develop long, strong legs for running away, either. Or claws, fangs, or other weapons for defending ourselves. We lived in perfect balance with the others on the island.

Until the tall chimps came sailing along. The small animals they brought with them, dogs and pigs, tore us apart. Those animals weren't the deadliest creatures who ever lived. But to us, they were deadly enough. Unable to run or fly, we were easy feasts.

But we were even more easily devoured by the tall chimps themselves. Whenever one of them felt like a snack, he just picked up a stick and thwacked a dodo on the head. No struggle. No chase. No chance. Less than a century after the tall chimps came to our island, the entire dodo species was gone from the planet.

Except for me.

For some reason, I never vanished into the emptiness of space like the rest of you. Maybe it's because the death of my species was so swift. Or because my incredible anger weighs me down. But over the centuries since my death, I've been left to drift across the surface of the planet, watching, studying, observing in horror . . . as tall chimps do to one species after another what they did to the dodo.

Empowered by their ferocious brains, they can catch and kill any creature they want. If they decide to hunt a certain animal, it's as good as dead—and its entire species will probably soon be in danger of extinction. For example, some tall chimps like to snack on the fins of frowning fish. So the frowning fish species is in danger of being wiped out.

But they hunt down creatures for many other reasons than just to feed themselves. They hunt those big mammoths to use the tusks as trinkets. They hunt other species for materials they wear or build with or rub on their flesh. Whatever the reason, if they want a part of your body, your species is in danger of disappearing.

> ***"Empowered
> by their ferocious brains,
> they can catch and kill any
> creature they want."***

But most of their killing they do without trying, or even being aware. They just move into an area to make their homes or raise their food, and a whole system on which countless creatures depend is knocked out of whack. Seems like everywhere they go, they cut down trees and other large plants that creatures need.

Sometimes they decide to kill off one particular creature that they consider a pest, and in the process kill members of a hundred other species. They leave a deadly mixture out that kills a pest . . . and then that kills a small animal that eats the dead pest, and a medium-sized animal that eats that dead small animal, and a large animal that eats the dead medium-sized animal . . .

They totally transform any region they move into with the deadly swiftness of a meteorite.

A century ago the planet was crawling with them. In another century it will be packed. And as the number of them soars, the number of other creatures plunges. Before they came along, a species went extinct about every thousand years. Now a species goes extinct about once an hour.

Though most of the dying species are small plants, plenty are animals. In a couple of decades, half of all large animals—including many keystone species—could be gone or on the way out. And you

*saw what happens when a keystone species goes: the whole
neighborhood goes, plants and animals alike.*

*How many groups of species can the planet stand to lose? Sure, it's a
big planet, and there are still millions of species. So no single species
is really missed at the moment. But when you take enough important
stones out of any structure, even the largest dam will come tumbling
down. Upset the balance in enough neighborhoods, and the entire
planet could end up unlivable.*

*Yes, even tall chimps themselves might soon be in danger. They won't
notice it at first. Maybe a few of their favorite plant snacks will be
scarce. Then a few of the animals they liked to wear will disappear.
Then they might notice the air getting filthy, since plants they've been
wiping out help keep the air clean.*

But soon the danger will be impossible to ignore.

*As one neighborhood after another dies, the air will get worse and
worse, causing other plants to die, which will cause other animals to
die, and other neighborhoods to fall, faster and faster, with each
cluster of extinctions triggering another, until there's no food for
anyone to eat, no air for anyone to breathe, no water for anyone to
drink, and the cycle of death has spun out of control.*

*There have been mass extinctions before, where most species living on
the planet at a particular time died out, over tens of thousands of
years. But the mass extinction now on the horizon could be the
swiftest and most complete of them all.*

*It could be the first mass extinction to leave the planet totally
uninhabitable. And it would definitely be the first mass extinction
caused by a single species.*

When Dodo finished we stood there frozen. Dazed.

Then we erupted. Fury overtook us like a wave.

Started dashing like crazy, we did. Without planning, without thinking. Right into this huge pack of tall chimps we tore, desperate to get them to change their ways.

I clung to Alticamelus' neck as he darted in front of a pack of tall chimps that must have been a hundred strong. To get their attention, the camel waved his neck so wildly that a weaker fella would have been thrown 10 miles.

Triceratops thundered ahead alongside Woolly, and those two yelped and yowled for all they were worth. Plesie plopped herself right down in front of a stream of tall chimps cruising ahead in their contraptions. Flapped and squealed she did, contorting her neck every which way.

Meg swooped over a crowd, as Dryo hung from her belly by his feet, shaking his fists and shouting down at his cousins. Rex clambered up a towering structure, shimmying 100 feet into the sky, blasting the tall chimps inside with bloodcurdling roars. Saber-tooth pounced in all directions, anxious to knock down tall chimps, grip them in his paws, and shake some sense into them.

But we're just ghosts. Those tall chimps couldn't feel our paws, see our fists, or hear our cries. We just drifted right on through the whole chimp-packed area. Right on through the crowds. Right on through the structures. Right on into a field, where we sat, all exhausted and flustered.

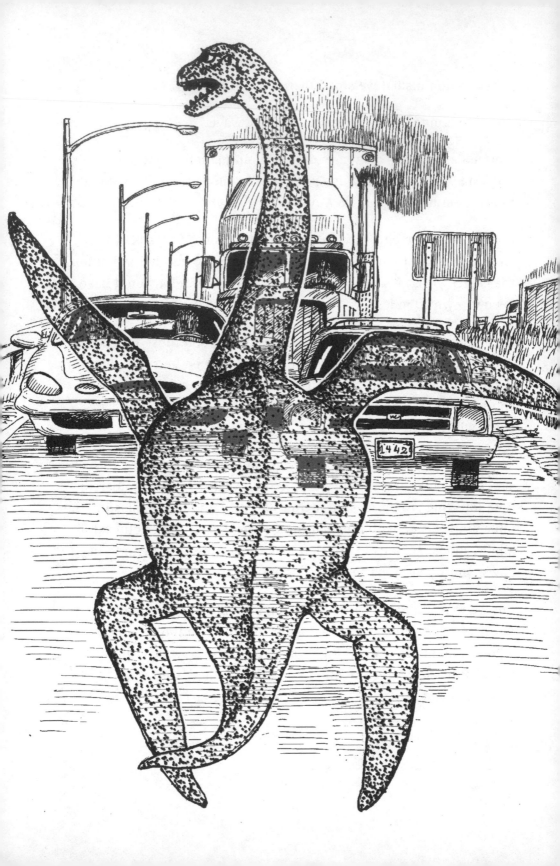

Sure looked as if Dodo had won the bet. As if all our relatives were on the way out and our old home planet would be as cold and empty as all the others. As if life would soon be a thing of the past. As if there would never be another reunion, because there would be no place to visit.

And wouldn't you know it, we couldn't even grieve in peace without being interrupted by a bunch of . . . you-know-whats.

"Isn't it absolutely nauseating?" said Alticamelus. "Just look at those tall chimps thoughtlessly scattering their used materials all over the grass, where it's sure to crush plants and poison animals."

Then I noticed something that made my eyes nearly pop right out of my head. "Look again!" I told Alticamelus.

What we were watching was as strange as watching a fish swim backwards through a stream. Or a tiger leap twenty feet backwards through the air. Or a long-necked dinosaur reach his head up into a tree and spit leaves back onto the branches.

"Those tall chimps aren't tossing their used materials down," I announced, "they're picking them up!"

Chapter 11

I WAS EXHAUSTED AFTER UNLOADING THE SECRET I'D BEEN carrying for centuries. So when Megazostrodon asked us to look carefully at a bunch of tall chimps, I really didn't have the energy. Or the stomach.

But he insisted there was something different about these particular tall chimps. And when I checked, I realized he was right: they were shorter than most of the others.

But that wasn't the only odd thing about them. It was their behavior. In all my years of observing the species, I'd never noticed any like these. They were doing the exact opposite of what normal tall chimps do!

I figured they were mutants—members of a species who end up with an unexpected trait. A lot of the time, mutants are unable to perform the functions members of their species need to do to survive. So they stagger around, struggle, and die alone.

But these mutant tall chimps weren't alone. There were dozens of them, gathering the scattered materials until the field was totally clean. Could this be a perverse strain of tall chimps devoted to un–tall-chimpifying the planet?

Our interest was aroused. So we followed the mutants as they got into a rolling beast that took them to . . .

An artificial world! Here creatures from around the globe lived in environments carefully crafted to mimic nature. In a way, this strange series of settings was a tiny version of the world as it used to be, inhabited by a tremendous variety of creatures living in the wild. Of course, it was all a sham. There was always some fence, some wall, something, however disguised, keeping the creatures imprisoned.

If tall chimps like to view these creatures, why don't they take the trouble to go see them in their natural habitats? I wondered. But as we continued to explore I realized that finding some of these creatures in their natural habitats would be almost impossible. I hadn't seen them for decades—because they were nearly extinct.

In one area set up to look like a jungle, we saw a sluggish tiger just lying there by himself. With white patches around his eyes, a round face, and a white belly striped with black, this lonely creature was a type of tiger that I thought had already disappeared. He'd better get used to loneliness, I thought. He's probably the last surviving member of his species.

I was wrong! A tall chimp led a second member of this rare tiger type into the setting. But if the tall chimps were hoping to solve the tiger's loneliness problem, nice try. Not feeling the least bit comfortable in her new home, the visitor dashed into a corner. The first tiger didn't seem to like having his space invaded either; he scampered into a cave. So much for members of one species picking mates for members of another.

But in another area, one of these forced couplings had done better. Members of an endangered species of chubby chimps had become comfortable enough with their artificial setting to raise a family. They scampered around, ignorant of the fact that their safe, comfortable, leafy home was a carefully crafted gift from their primate cousins.

As I took in the scene, something about these tall chimps' behavior began to confuse me. An observation by Megazostrodon increased my confusion.

"Would you look at this tall chimp's feet?" he called, skittering across the feet of a particular tall chimp whose feet were covered with what seemed to be lizard skin.

"The hypocrisy," Triceratops railed. "Coming to observe members of one endangered species, while wearing the skin of members of another."

"But it's not skin," Megazostrodon insisted. And he was right! As Triceratops studied the material, she realized that the tall chimp's feet were covered with some kind of lizard-skin substitute.

"Well, how do you like that?" yelped Woolly. "They've figured out how to make a fur substitute, too!" She had found a tall chimp clad in a material that looked like wild cat fur, was as thick as fur, and as warm—but clearly wasn't fur.

Weird!

My brain began to race. Could some tall chimps actually have a clue? Could they be aware of the danger? Could they be willing to make a special effort to keep endangered species from dying out?

My thoughts about the tall chimps outside the settings made me wonder . . . about just what the tall chimps inside were really up to.

Could it possibly be? I wondered. Could these tall chimps actually be trying to rescue these species from extinction? Could they really realize the trouble these species are in, and care? And understand the importance of each species in the grand scheme of things?

Could it be that these creatures, who had done so much to upset the balance of life, were now trying to restore it?

"If that's what they're trying to do, it's a pretty pathetic attempt," said Saber-tooth, after I shared my musings with the group. "Tigers need enormous areas to live in. We keep strong by stalking our food and fighting for it, not having it handed to us."

"I think it's incredible!" said Dryopithecus, quick to grab onto any sign of hope. "My cousins have figured out how to make up for their little goofs! They've found a way to save any species that's in trouble—even if there are only two members left! And now they're going to get each endangered species back on its feet, one at a time, 'til the planet's teeming with wildlife again!"

"Sorry if I can't share your optimism, Dryo," said Alticamelus, "but when it gets to the point where there are only two members of a species left, it's too late. A species needs a lot of members to survive. That way, with changes in the environment or new diseases, *some* of the members will survive and continue the species. Even if there are thousands of members of a species left, it might be too late to save the entire species."

"But I wouldn't put anything past these tall chimps," protested Megazostrodon. "Sharpest creatures I've seen in all my days, they are. And, as the top mammals, they come from a long line of survivors."

"It doesn't matter how smart they are, or how hard they try," said Woolly. "They can use their brains to make real fine contraptions that do a hundred million different things. They can even make contraptions that cruise like animals, or fly like animals. But even these geniuses can't create animals from scratch. Once a species is gone, it's gone."

"Maybe they can't create animals from scratch right now," argued Rex. "But let's not underrate these guys. According to what you yourself said, Woolly, only a few thousand years ago their mightiest weapon was a club! They're getting smarter and stronger with incredible speed. Before long they'll be rearranging the stars. Remember, they're the most powerful creatures ever to walk the planet."

"Exactly," said Triceratops angrily, "and for thousands of years now they've been directing that tremendous power against other creatures. Against nature itself. That's exactly why it's too late."

"Way too late," echoed Plesie. "All over the planet, the awful process they've set in motion is moving swiftly along. From the deepest sea, to the coral reefs, to the jungles, to the deserts, even on the highest mountains. A mass extinction is coming that no creatures will survive."

"Bugs will survive," Meganeura piped up. "We're adaptable. We're tough. There are so many different kinds, some of us are bound to make it through the coming mass extinction. In fact, maybe once the large mammals go, we'll take over! Like the mammals did after the dinosaurs fell! I bet that at our next reunion, bugs the size of dinosaurs will be running the place!"

"What do *you* think?" Woolly asked, turning to me. "What'll our planet be like tomorrow? Will it be covered with nothing but bugs? Or will it be swarming with tall chimps, who keep all the other species squished into a few fake settings? Will our relatives be rescued, and keep on growing and evolving, 'til the planet is teeming with all kinds of new species? Or will there be no species at all, no water, no air, just a dry old dead floating rock?"

> ## "Could these tall chimps actually be trying to rescue these species from extinction?"

"In other words, Dodo," said Alticamelus quietly, "who wins the bet?"

The others waited, listening for my answer. And so I thought. I thought of how the planet had been transformed in the centuries since my death—how countless species that had slowly developed and adapted over millions of years were carelessly wiped out in the process.

I thought of all the species on their way to being wiped out, and how important many of these species were to the survival of others. I thought about how a few tall chimps seemed to realize the danger, of the tremendous power they, and they alone, had to change things. And I thought of how little time might be left for them to act.

All these thoughts jumbled around in my mind, until my answer became clear. I realized what I had to say, and so I said it: "I just don't know."

The final act

AS THE SUN BEGAN TO SET ON THE ZOO, THE CHILDREN
reboarded the bus and departed. The animal ghosts
also departed, returning to the field where they had
first appeared.

When the ghosts had congregated on the field, they began to
embrace. They embraced in pairs. And in clusters. Finally, all the
ghosts, from the towering Tyrannosaurus to the tiny Megazostrodon,
from the furry Mammoth to the scaly Triceratops, from the winged
Meganeura to the flipper-clad Plesiosaur, from the long-necked
Alticamelus to the fanged Saber-tooth to even the squat Dodo, joined
in a single group embrace.

As their forms began to fade, the ghosts relaxed their grip on one
another and seemed to embrace the planet. One ghost brushed its
fur against the bark of a tree, another rubbed its belly across the
grass, one thrust its snout into a bush, another dug its teeth into a
root, and another scraped its claws across the surface of the dirt . . .
as though believing they could actually feel these things.

Within an instant, the ghosts had vanished into the darkness of
space.

All was still for a moment. Then a stray dog pranced across the field
carrying a sneaker in its mouth. A squirrel, startled by the dog,
scurried into its hole as, overhead, a pair of birds flitted from a
telephone pole into a tree, chirping their tuneful, cryptic messages.

Cast of characters

Geologic time divisions

Epoch Any of several divisions of a geological period.

Period A division of geologic time longer than an epoch and included in an era.

Era A stage in development; one of the four major divisions in geologic time.

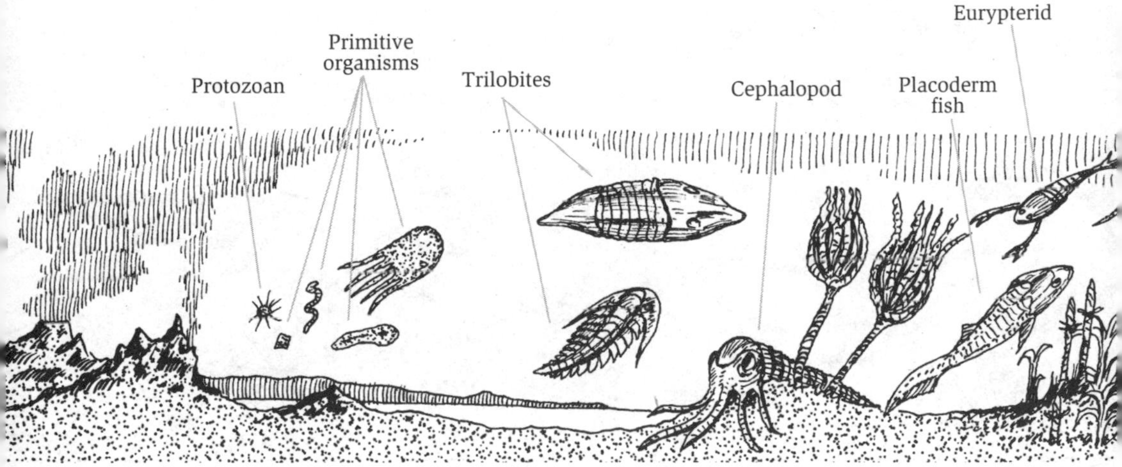

Eurypterid

Primitive
organisms

Protozoan

Trilobites

Cephalopod

Placoderm
fish

ARCHEOZOIC PERIOD	PROTEROZOIC PERIOD	CAMBRIAN PERIOD	ORDOVICIAN PERIOD

PRECAMBRIAN ERA

PALEOZOIC ERA
The Age of Amphibians

Earth's crust solidified	Primitive aquatic plants	Trilobites	First fishes
Earliest life forms	Bacteria	Brachiopods	Seaweeds
Blue-green algae	Algae		Fungi

3.5 billion
years ago

2.5 billion
years ago

600 million
years ago

500 million
years ago

425 million
years ago

Meganeura The world's largest known flying insect, meganeura was the size of a small sea gull. It lived about 300 million years ago, during the Carboniferous period, when much of the earth was covered by moist, swampy forests. If meganeura's life cycle was like that of the modern dragonfly, as scientists believe, this ancient insect lived near water and laid its eggs on the surface of lakes and swamps.

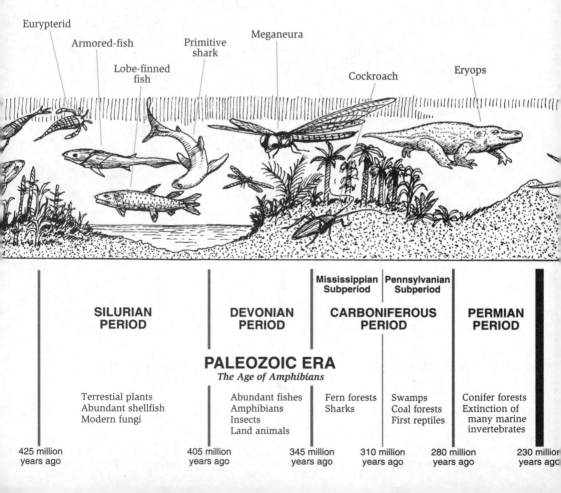

Eurypterid

Armored-fish

Lobe-finned fish

Primitive shark

Meganeura

Cockroach

Eryops

			Mississippian Subperiod	Pennsylvanian Subperiod	
SILURIAN PERIOD	**DEVONIAN PERIOD**	**CARBONIFEROUS PERIOD**			**PERMIAN PERIOD**

PALEOZOIC ERA
The Age of Amphibians

Terrestial plants	Abundant fishes	Fern forests	Swamps	Conifer forests
Abundant shellfish	Amphibians	Sharks	Coal forests	Extinction of
Modern fungi	Insects		First reptiles	many marine
	Land animals			invertebrates

| 425 million years ago | 405 million years ago | 345 million years ago | 310 million years ago | 280 million years ago | 230 million years ago |

Plesiosaur An aquatic reptile that could be up to 40 feet long, the plesiosaur lived between 200 and 65 million years ago. Though there were several plesiosaur species, most had long necks, short tails, and flippers. The plesiosaur is believed to have been a swift, skilled swimmer—like the dolphin and seal of today—and to have been a meat eater, surviving on a diet of fish and other sea animals. Don't be fooled by the name; the plesiosaur was not a dinosaur, since true dinosaurs lived on land.

Megazostrodon One of the earliest mammals, megazostrodon lived between 200 and 135 million years ago, when dinosaurs ruled the earth. Scientists believe this 4-inch-long mammal hid among plants during the day to avoid being eaten by chicken-sized meat-eating dinosaurs, only coming out at night to satisfy its own appetite for small lizards, insects, and mammals.

Triceratops A 25-foot-long plant eater, the triceratops lived at the same time as the tyrannosaurus. With a name meaning "three-horn-face," the triceratops had two large horns above its eyes and a smaller horn on its snout. In addition, it had a large, hard crest around its neck that helped protect this vulnerable region from large meat eaters.

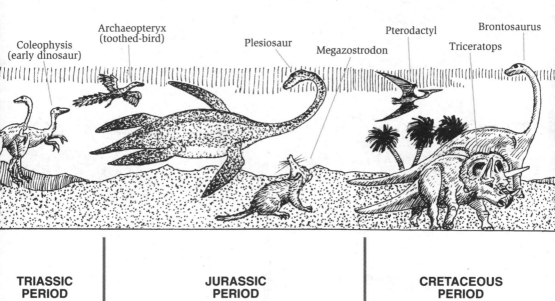

Coleophysis (early dinosaur)

Archaeopteryx (toothed-bird)

Plesiosaur

Megazostrodon

Pterodactyl

Triceratops

Brontosaurus

TRIASSIC PERIOD	JURASSIC PERIOD	CRETACEOUS PERIOD

MESOZOIC ERA
The Age of Reptiles

First dinosaurs	First birds	Climax of dinosaurs
Cycads	First mammals	and extinction
Active volcanoes	Flying reptiles	Modern insects
	Ammonites	Flowering plants

190 million years ago

140 million years ago

Tyrannosaurus rex The tyrannosaurus lived between 75 and 65 million years ago. An adult of this species was about 20 feet tall, weighed about 5 tons, and had teeth nearly a foot long, which it used to tear apart and devour other large dinosaurs. Its name means "king of the lizards." Tyrannosaurus had long been considered the largest meat-eating land animal that ever lived, but two recent discoveries in Argentina and Africa have uncovered two even larger dinosaurs. Gigantosaurus and Carcharodontosaurus or "shark-toothed lizard" are slightly larger than Tyrannosaurus rex.

Alticamelus Ancestor of the modern camel, the alticamelus lived in North America about 19 million years ago. Though most of its body resembled a camel's, the alticamelus's long neck made it look like a cross between a camel and a giraffe. Since it stood about 10 feet tall, the alticamelus is believed to have fed on higher tree leaves, as a giraffe does.

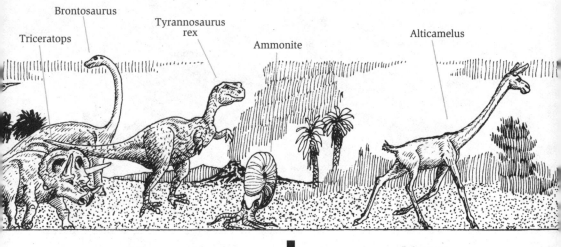

Brontosaurus

Triceratops

Tyrannosaurus rex

Ammonite

Alticamelus

Paleocene
Epoch

**CRETACEOUS
PERIOD**

MESOZOIC ERA
The Age of Reptiles

Mild to cool climate
Primates
First placental
  mammals

65 million
years ago

Dryopithecus An ancestor of the human being, dryopithecus belonged to a group of primates that lived between 25 and 10 million years ago. Though it looked a lot like a chimpanzee, its shorter arms gave it a somewhat more human appearance. With a name meaning "tree ape," dryopithecus is believed to have lived in India, Africa, and Europe.

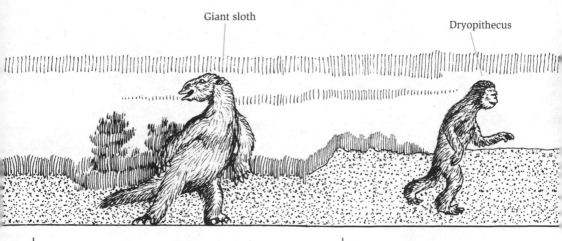

Giant sloth

Dryopithecus

Eocene Epoch	Oligocene Epoch

TERTIARY PERIOD

CENOZOIC ERA
The Age of Mammals

Warm climate
Giant birds
Modern types
  of mammals

Large running
mammals

55 million
years ago

40 million
years ago

Saber-toothed tiger A cat slightly larger than a lion, the saber-toothed tiger lived between 1.3 million and 12 thousand years ago. With its pair of 9-inch teeth, or "sabers," the cat could stab and kill such prey as ground sloths and mammoths, especially when these creatures became trapped in tar pits or marshes. The saber-toothed tiger's formal name is "smilodon."

Woolly mammoth The ancestor of the modern elephant, the woolly mammoth lived between 1.3 million and 10 thousand years ago. The thick, woolly hair that covered its body served to protect the mammoth from the intense cold of the Ice Age. Since actual bodies of woolly mammoths have been found frozen in ice, scientists can be certain of the color of its fur, which ranged from reddish-brown to dark brown. Early Native Americans hunted the mammoth for food.

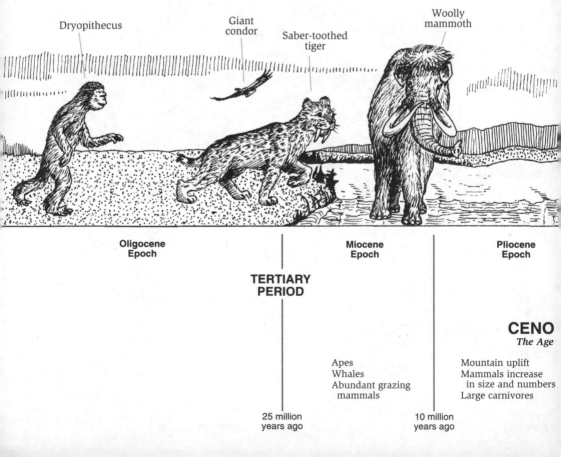

Dryopithecus

Giant condor

Saber-toothed tiger

Woolly mammoth

Oligocene Epoch		Miocene Epoch		Pliocene Epoch

TERTIARY PERIOD

CENO
The Age

		Apes		Mountain uplift
		Whales		Mammals increase
		Abundant grazing		in size and numbers
		mammals		Large carnivores

25 million years ago

10 million years ago

Dodo A large, flightless bird, the dodo became extinct only a few centuries ago. Though different species of dodo lived on various islands, it was the species that lived on the island of Mauritius that has become famous as a symbol for extinction. Since there were no predators on its island, the dodo didn't evolve skills that would enable it to defend itself. So when human explorers discovered Mauritius in the late 1500s, they found the defenseless bird an easy catch—and a highly desirable one, since its 50 pounds of meat was enough to feed an entire ship's crew. Besides killing dodos themselves, human visitors brought pigs and rats that preyed on the dodo's eggs. Within 70 years of the arrival of humans on Mauritius, the dodo was extinct.

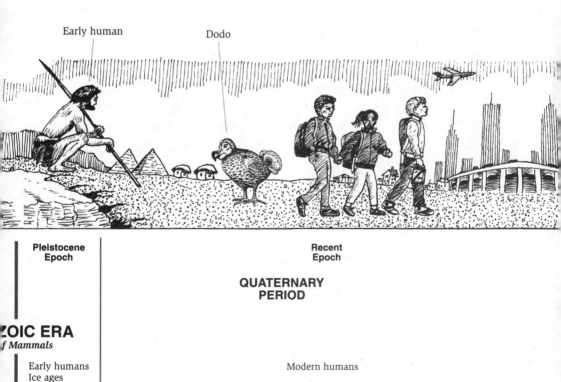

Early human

Dodo

Pleistocene Epoch	Recent Epoch

QUATERNARY PERIOD

ʑOIC ERA
f Mammals

Early humans
Ice ages

Modern humans

.7 million
ears ago

10,000
years ago

About the author

Billy Aronson   A thin, flightless human, the Billy Aronson has
written two books published by W.H. Freeman: *They Came from DNA*,
which was named an NSTA/CBC Outstanding Book for Children in
1994, and *Scientific Goofs*, which has been translated into Turkish
and Chinese. He is also a playwright, with a play featured in
Best American Short Plays 1992-93 (Applause Books), and lyrics
featured in the musical *Rent*, for which he is also credited with the
original concept. To feed his offspring, the Billy writes for television.

About the illustrator

John Quinn   Among the most versatile of mammals, the John Quinn has been known to transport himself by cycling, canoeing, snorkeling, scuba diving, or even walking on two feet. Over the past three and a half decades, the John has been an artist and a naturalist, working at such scientific institutions as the Academy of Natural Science (Philadelphia), the New England Aquarium (Boston), and the American Museum of Natural History (New York). He has also written over a dozen science books. John is a direct ancestor of his five daughters and grandson.